Bards, Robots, and Hordes

Hank Youngman

2024

The following text is an informal essay. Parts have been fictionalized in varying degrees, for various purposes. The text is meant as literary entertainment only. The author bears no responsibility for any further inferences on the part of the reader. Citations and paraphrased text by other authors have been credited according to the MLA citation guidelines.

List of Contents

Battle Hymn of the Defeated

<u>Deceived with Ornament</u>

It was not that long ago that I began writing *Pythagoras' Prison*. It was the first essay in this series, at once an introduction and a spinoff, and with it, I hoped to address what I perceived has been the unspoken maxim of the time, which, in the nature of unspoken maxims, makes up the contemporary fallacy – not by itself, but first as a symptom, and, in the vicious cycle of deception, as a major contributor: the worship of numbers. Indeed, numbers have come to dominate science, politics, and the things we value: not only are the humanities disregarded because they have little concern for numbers, but they have tried to cope with this by forcing quantitative studies at the expense of their theoretical wealth; in business, statistics are the be-all and the end-all of decisions, humanity be damned; in regards to human values, it is the measurable dimension, i.e. measurable on a scalar system, that takes precedence over anything else: success is the money a man makes, beauty is the size of a woman's bust, right and wrong are mob-inheritance. If space is the final frontier, then numbers are the final authority: mysterious and imposing and at the same time malleable to the whims of whoever gets to count, they are the ideal god of our godless world – impersonal, amoral, yet infinite: infinitely plentiful, infinitely impressive, and infinitely vague. If you have read *Pythagoras' Prison*, you already understand the unflattering nature of the problem.

It is in consistency with this that I now concede what a failure it must have been, my essay. Its poor sales never a concern, for numbers mean little to me in regards to success, I had to accept that my message must not have inspired the kind of thought it ought to have, as I saw, just before beginning this chapter, a woman, a young and prosperous gorgeous woman with tastefully applied makeup and meticulously styled hair, talking, in an attractive a manner as the subject warrants, about the oppression of womankind in patriarchal modernity, bring up the argument that *research has proven, time and again, that women are more competent statesmen than men.* She followed this up with a tangent, claiming that it is pointless for men to argue that, though some men may be chauvinists or rapists or racists, most of us are none of those things, for we do nothing to alter the fact that, regardless of the civilized majority,[1] members of the feminine gender are nonetheless treated as second-class citizens. The statistics on the matter, she said, were irrefutable. This was a conversation broadcast (on television) across the nation. I take it that what she had to say must have been a subject deemed worthy of the ears of this same unfortunate nation. I think the reader can now see why, at the moment of writing this, I consider *Pythagoras' Prison* to have been unsuccessful in its purpose – no minds have been changed, at least to no level worthy of public consideration. Not only did our nascent intellectual mount a chiefly numeric assault, but, to make things worse, it was somewhat of a middle finger to my central essay, thus turning two out of two published essays into flops, seeing as her subject of choice was as intellectually cheap as it has been conversationally exhausted. Long past sincere interest, the gender-wars rage without a sign of stopping, and it is statistics that are to determine the victor – consenting or otherwise.

Now, I write this with the self-consciousness of a melodramatic wannabe: I understand that there is no reason for me to expect anybody, let alone a public intellectual such as herself, to have read my books or to have agreed with their message or to ever know that there exists such a thing as a Youngman (or his books). Being the second-class citizen that she obviously is, our modern prodigy has more important things on her mind, like her makeup and her appearance on television, not to mention she has her hands full with her NGO. But I also say these things with the conviction that there is nothing immorally melodramatic in arguing that such a state of affairs is a problem. It is a double standard that, though I

---

[1] her argument, not mine.

should feel ashamed for expecting anybody to entertain my thoughts, given the multitudes of people in the world and the multitudes of problems they face (none of them related to what I have to say), I should also feel ashamed for not entertaining the thoughts of people like her – of attractive, successful second-class citizens with rather sonorous last names, that tell me things quite unrelated to the problems that I face. It goes for anybody and everybody: it is considered normal that we remain ignored; we are even encouraged to ignore one another – however, we must not dare be ignorant of specific people, whose interests, though uninteresting, have been proclaimed as superior to our own.

Men are being marginalized. Society is fine with that. Individual women are also being marginalized. Society is generally fine with that as well. There are too many of us for everybody to care about anybody. Did I not write that "It is extinction most mandatory / that one means but one in seven billion" (*Chapbooks* 105)? Just a bit earlier, I had written that, unable to become the 1%, we try to imitate the 1% – that our aspirations have to do with

> being a smaller percentage within the multitude, and thus achieving a uniqueness by proxy – a degradation of the 99% such that they became but a set of unrelated digits, singular ones scattered across ninety-nine places, united in misery and kept separate by ambition (*Playwright* 16).

Nobody matters to anybody; each man an atom upon himself, floating around in the cluster of methane we collectively make up, never noticing the dung to which our essence restrains us. And yet, despite this mutual indifference, assumed as another unspoken social contract, there are successful and attractive men and successful and attractive second-class citizens every day on the news, there being behind every one of them another successful and attractive man or successful and attractive second-class citizen, speaking boldly and assuredly and (do not be mistaken) correctly and justly and without any possibility to err, regarding whom ignorance is a sin, and regarding whom criticism is in all cases projection, a side effect of frustration (no doubt at one's underachievement – no doubt deserved). Criticism of people not quite as prevalent in the media, by contrast, is a mere matter-of-fact, being unwashed as they fancy we must be, and as unpopular as we are destined to remain. We have been denied historical recognition as individual persons with individual personalities by the men and the second-class citizens that govern us, culminating, as far as I can see, in a retroactive oblivion: to live as if we never were. This, we are told, we must accept; the opposite is an ego-problem.

Joke aside, this ought to be discouraging: one cannot be heard unless one's voice has been approved by an authority, be it an authority with wealth or an authority rich in decibels, of which the former have tastes of *peculiar* character, and the latter have no taste at all; the privilege of being heard is reserved but for the spineless and the incult. And yet, I interpret this as a fundamentally good sign: to encounter opposition of this scope, opposition that, to one's advances responds with the harshest of intellectual penalties – isolation – cannot be but proof of fighting the right battle: the battle for the most heavily fortified stronghold, and so of a disproportionally powerful enemy; one willing to govern who gets to be heard and what gets to be uttered and at last agreed upon. To add to my conviction, there is the fact that what I speak of is a battle waged, in all likelihood, since history has been there to record it.

In Bassanio's speech in Act III by which he wins Portia's hand in marriage, a speech that, if you are interested in autobiographical trivia, earned me that same nickname in my freshman year, Shakespeare's side-character begins his iconic lines like so: "So may the outward shows be least themselves / The world is still deceived with ornament" (3.2 75-76). The ornament in question is anything that holds no truth in itself but fancy makes appear important – wealth, rhetoric (77-82), status, tradition (85-90), beauty (90-98), you name it. "There is no vice so simple but assumes / Some mark of virtue on his outward parts" (83-84). Written over four hundred years before the present day, this speech records deception by ornament as an ongoing affair – something out of which, according to its sixteenth-century narrator, the world should have long since grown out. It is a historically correct use of the adverb, in as far as it is a problem of which Socrates and his peers were also well-aware. Diogenes Laertius mentions, on the subject of physical beauty, that "Aristotle... defined good looks as the gift of god, Socrates as a short-lived reign, Plato as natural superiority, Theophrastus as a mute deception, Theocritus as an evil in an ivory setting, Carneades as a monarchy that needs no bodyguard." Moreover, you do not need me to tell you that elitism was common when nepotism was a virtue. Evidently, the deception Shakespeare poeticized can be traced all the way back to antiquity. It can also be traced to modernity. The key word remains *still*.

All this leads me to conclude that I am fighting a fight that, as boring as it is on the surface, is really epic in both its scope and its agelessness. If it was a problem for Shakespeare and if it was a problem for Socrates, then there is something over which both myself and my indifferent critic (not even bothering to address me directly) should feel ashamed to some degree: myself, that I ever hoped to circumvent a problem that proved an obstacle to people much wiser than myself, and my critic, that he should ever call my displeasure at this state of affairs reactionary rage or a coping mechanism or an egoic delusion or any other pseudointellectual slur, when it has been a perfectly real conflict between the privileged and the marginalized long before either myself or my disinterested critic came into existence – whatever my reaction, it is neither contrived nor fallacious; the world remains deceived by ornament. To think this a minor affair is to live in ignorance not just of an angry individual in the present day, but to be ignorant of a continuous struggle in history.

I am not sure exactly what the critic should do to address this – except change his attitude entirely, which I doubt he will. Myself, however, I know exactly what it means for me: as I write, and as you read (Dear Reader, this applies to you no less than it applies to me), I must allow that, though my initial motive has been the satisfaction of an urge to intellectualize, whatever frustration I have set out to vent, arguably selfishly at first, has led us to the field of an ageless struggle. It is only moral, now that we're here, to join the ranks of the good side – the one that does not believe in such a thing as a *my place* or *your place* that is any different from the place of any other honest citizen.

Lacking any guarantee of success, my decision is at once reckless and bold, but not exactly self-flattering, as the labor needed to write non-fiction is not at all welcoming to a self-serving character. Nor am I deterred by labor without guaranteed payment. Payment is also a bad ornament if we confuse it for the ultimate goal of our legacy. I persist in what I do, sharing a conviction with those minds whose opinions I respect. It is the only nourishment my cause requires, and a kind of reward not at all appealing to the careless or the spineless or their enablers. I would rather partake in the aspirations of the men I value than chase after the ornaments of men with no concern for value.

G.K. Chesterton – a Daymare

One of my Bill and Ted fantasies revolves around a man large enough, in metaphor and in girth, to have his own gravitational pull, and so have many things revolve around him. The irony being that there are very few things that do revolve around that uncheated prophet of modernity; most people, even most well-read people, have never heard of him or his works, though they know many other writers of significantly lesser talent. This is a consequence of the circularity that plagues formal literary schooling, but that is a subject for another chapter.

Chesterton was an English writer, known for his controversial views regarding common sense, namely the extreme position that it is an important thing on which to rely. Throughout his opus, like an outspoken conservative mind, he emphasizes his theistic worldview, and, like a revolutionary liberal mind, he expresses his disgust with capitalism. This has disqualified him from both camps. One might be tempted to call him a rebel as a result, however, I would warn against it, for he appears to have disliked that designation.[2] Now that I have established a basic identity for our protagonist, I will conclude the paragraph with a reminder to the reader that part of the fun of a Bill and Ted fantasy is the fish-out-of-water effect concerning the historical figure of choice, and it is precisely for this reason that I hold Chesterton an ideal candidate for an evocation in modernity: a man from the past must experience the future with a degree of disagreement, else it is no fun.

Regarding Chesterton, I used to wonder if he would be so happy at seeing the future, that he would pay little mind to the crises that have emerged in the meantime. I know I would in his place. There would be too much culture to ponder on its downfall. Then again, in order to understand much of it, he would need to know the history of everything that has happened between his time and the present, and, with that, acute outrage sounds like the likelier reaction. This is especially true if one considers how much of Chesterton's work contains criticism of western economy and eugenics, which seem to have developed exactly as he predicted. This raises yet another possibility, and that is the reaction of prophetic pride: he called it as he saw it, and he saw it as it was bound to happen; it is a flattering thought, to have the privilege of a century-enduring *I-told-you-so* in an intellectual matter.

But I suspect I have been overthinking things again. I have been looking at it from the wrong perspective. Remember, it is important that the character should approach the future with a

---

[2] "They will be only too pleased to be able to say that we, by our own confession, are merely restless and negative; that we are only what we call rebels and they call cranks. But it is not true... I should not say to Mr. Rockefeller 'I am a rebel.' I should say 'I am a respectable man: and you are not'" ("The New Name").

fish-out-of-water mentality. Perhaps Mr. Chesterton would not be quite as interested in the socio-political climate of the present day, nor in the history that followed his time on Earth, but rather, his immediate inquiry would be of something regarding his immediate surroundings. In this sense, it is perhaps best to assume that his first opinion on modernity would be an opinion on the visible differences between then and now. To the modern mind, this is no doubt technology.

If it were up to me, I would first show him the good side of our gizmos and gadgets. I would not like him to get the impression that it is all bad, only to see that I own all of it – this thing that is all bad. It is with this intention that I would first let him know about the dictionary application on my phone, the reading app, with which I am allowed a library of classics at my fingertips, all the beautiful music on the device, the contacts I have been able to keep, and the camera with which I have captured many memorable moments – made all the livelier with the quality of the pictures, not least their sharing and the compliments they have received online. That the dictionary has made me less interested in learning new words as I can easily look them up now, that I seldom use the device to read, that all that beautiful music is of the past, that most of my contacts I do not contact, and that most of those shared pictures are not of especially sincere moments, are things of which I would inform him only after he has become acquainted with the benefits of technology.

My interest in his opinion on this matter in particular, I should note, is because I am almost positive it would not be what most of us tend to comment on the subject. We all peddle the same genre of wisdom: *technology is neither good nor bad, but a neutral (or amoral) collection of inventions that can be either directed to one end or twisted to another, and it is up to us as individuals to decide whether a smartphone is a learning device or an ego-machine.* But not Chesterton. Our hero's reply would be a unique contribution, that is at once a common-sense truism and a truth hidden from the true commoner, senseless as he is.

It is according to my most reliable imagination that this prophet of an Englishman would consider the device, pretend to be taken aback by how much things have changed, and at last conclude that it is proof that nothing has changed at all. *People now carry the world in their pockets, he might say, and yet they are as simple as ever. Why wouldn't they be? To fit the world in your trousers is not a triumph of invention, but a triumph of ignorance – you have made the big small, and so, you have made all there is to learn into so little that needs learning.* I back this up with what he has said earlier regarding the shrinkage of the world.[3] The lines he utters next would be no less intelligent, and just as subversive for the normative thinker. *But how is this technology proof of change when the only thing it has proven is that nothing that actually matters is at all susceptible to change? You say that, on your mobile device, you can learn and read and photograph your happy moments, listen to good music and interact with your friends, which is good, and yet, it has made people lazy and vain and fake, which is bad. Is this supposed to be a novel development? For all it serves, it is to confirm that learning and camaraderie and good music are good things, and that laziness and fakery and ignorance are not. Show me something that has successfully argued to the contrary, and I will call your future a future marking a significant deviation from the past. Until then, we remain in antiquity, and it seems that it is where mankind is destined to remain: good is good, evil is evil, and it will always be so.* He would conclude this with an argument that attests for the reason he is disliked by self-proclaimed liberals and western conservatives alike. *Evil will always be evil, he would repeat, and as such, there is no such thing as a lesser evil, though you have convinced yourselves that some evil is*

---

[3] "It is inspiriting without doubt to whizz in a motor-car round the earth, to feel Arabia as a whirl of sand or China as a flash of rice-fields. But Arabia is not a whirl of sand and China is not a flash of rice-fields. They are ancient civilizations with strange virtues buried like treasures...To conquer these places is to lose them. The man standing in his own kitchen-garden, with fairyland opening at the gate, is the man with large ideas. His mind creates distance; the motor-car stupidly destroys it" (*Heretics*).

necessary for goodness. There is no such thing as an evil committed in the name of the good. Do not misinterpret medicine to prove me wrong. It is in bad taste. Painful medical procedures are not an evil endured for the sake of the good – they are rather good for the sake of the good, with pain being but an unpleasant side-effect, itself in no way evil, let alone a necessary evil. The only creatures I know to consider evil a necessity are subjects of demonology. To drop bombs on people in the name of securing peace is a wicked contradiction, not a tough decision – as if there is any toughness in having somebody else die in your stead. To the people you have killed, you will have inflicted the opposite of peace, and you will have become no less of a monster for whatever story you tell yourself to justify it. Evil, meaning corruption – meaning decay, has it in its nature to spread until it rots away with the foundation it infects; an evil allowed to take place will grow, by many factors (such as normalization and legislation and social inertia) and, even if it seems lesser in scope at the moment, it will become, uncontested as it is, the ultimate rot. Chesterton has become somewhat acquainted with modern history as he rounds off his argument. I admit, his lexicon contains words he may not have normally used, though, keep in mind, he might have picked them up looking at my phone.

*

I like to believe that we are not quite so far gone as to continue sinking, along with our costly fallacy. I write these books with the intention of putting my labor where my mouth is, seeing as I do not have the funds to do it without the written pages. Good, Dear Reader, however you choose to define it, will remain good. Evil will remain evil as long as it is allowed to exist. Please do not dismiss my essay (the tolerance of which is, I believe, a litmus test for the receptivity of the reader's mind) on account that I have begun (and will probably proceed) with ideas you may find disagreeable. There is a line between misunderstanding and hostility, and, as leniently as I like to reinterpret the latter, an iron curtain against a civil thought is an unmistakable sign of enmity.

Is it not a perverse tragedy that there is enmity between men on account of ideas? That brother turns against brother in the name of an exclusively speculative dimension? What idea could possibly be important enough to shut off one man from another, as if whatever its cause, no doubt, according to them, of noble conviction, is not cancelled out by the dismissal of one's own kin, reimagining oneself an alienating brute, regardless of the fantasy supporting the decision? Yet is it not borderline comedic, that if you are the kind to think in terms of *left and right*, you have no idea which side I am describing? To align to any idea so passionately as to place it above honest human interaction is not only a fallacy, but lunacy. We are meant to learn – not to convince ourselves that we have already learned all there is, that our opposition is evil, that our opponents are deceived, or that there is any enemy to reason other than the enemy to sincerity – which is true of any ideology by the way, when one mistakes it for the truth.

These are essays on human misunderstanding. That entails such a thing as the possibility to understand. Indeed, the positive has gone awry, but that is no excuse to let it remain that way. There is yet a chance to make things right. Never give in to an imposed narrative of fate. We have an obligation to oppose determinism. It is a moral duty for which discovery we are indebted to literary critics, for they have pointed to tragic predetermination as an essential motif in tragedy, which, not an external imposition upon the protagonists, stems from their tragic flaws. It is among the major characteristics by which the genre differs from both its highbrow opposite in comedy and its lowbrow complement in melodrama. Therefore, if we are to avoid either apocalyptic culpability or tastelessness, I stress, no matter the tyranny of fate, it is up to us to ensure we are not the characters that enable it. To let things unwind according to our imperfections is only to comply with the unhappy end of the world – the same that we all oppose with each breath, whether we know it or not.

It helps the indifferent reader little to say that he does not care about the world. To address him directly: the very fact that you live enrolls you in the project of existence – and you are in it for life. Your only choice right now is to either be good at it or prove useless in it. If that is a prospect that does not stir you to fight, I would not call you evil or stupid or anything quite as rude. I would only make note of you as a very determined liar – though a rather poor one, now that I think about it, being in your own deception the first to fall for it.

To the defeatists, if you have retained your interest in autobiographical tidbits, let me quickly quote from my sophomore nickname, and ask you whether, even if we allowed that "Let Hercules himself do what he may, / The cat will mew, and the dog will have his day" (5.1. 315), there is anybody among us who would rather be a canine or a feline instead of that mythic hero, futile though his feats may seem in retrospect? I would not be surprised if there are people who would. But let us not forget, there were at least two cats that did not mew after Hercules himself had done "what he may." One was at Cathaeron. The other was the Nemean lion. Therefore, the feats of Hercules, that mightiest of heroes, at once a vicious imbecile and a hero to boys worldwide, cannot have been entirely without merit. And neither are our own.

If even the Nemean lion's impenetrable skin eventually became ornamental hide, then an impenetrably thick skull must be somewhat receptive after all. No mind is perfectly immune to intelligent touch. Conversely, a *Nemean scalp* would only be good as ornamental hide – metaphorically, of course, to decorate with hair on one side and makeup on the other and carry around with the pride of a good catch. But if the latter is true of anyone, how little value must such a person hold, I fear to speculate publically. At least the lion's hide was supposed to have a practical use for Hercules, and it was impervious to the ravages of time. Its timelessness was, of course, because that incredible hide was a myth. In this world, things are not so: beauty is fleeting; status is temporary, and a trophy is just an unimaginative toy. The ornament one makes out of a thick head is not at all a quality ornament. Which is one reason I think that aging is a blessing. Advancing in age grants us access to two truths: first, that there is no permanence in fashionable values, and second, that there is yet a permanence to be observed in this life. And my imaginary time-travelling Chesterton has told us all about it.

In that sense, let us consider what stands in our way: misunderstanding. Now, let us study it and map it and determine what to do with it. I promise, it is surprisingly easy to overcome, once you have learned the difference between a dam and a buoy.

Two Types of Misunderstanding

I divide the sum of human misunderstandings in two great categories: misunderstandings of whim and misunderstandings of choice. I am only concerned with people struggling with the latter, as the former is a demographic of which I do not expect lasting results. Of the latter, I emphasize, this is only for people who struggle with it – those already entrenched in a misunderstanding of choice are impossible to dissuade.

The difference between misunderstandings of whim and misunderstandings of choice explains lapses in discipline, calculation, and personal accountability, and so not by positing the two expressions as a pair of moral antonyms, i.e. one presenting an absence of these attributes and the other their reclamation, but rather, as with diagnosing a medical condition, whether the issue is to be called chronic or acute.

I will ask the reader to consider the kind of friend who, upon conversing on a subject appears perfectly attentive, and so not because of his acting skills, but because he is genuinely interested in what you have to say; a subject on which he has paid little mind, but now hears elaborated with arguments he had until then not considered at all – he is surprised it is even possible to speak this way on the matter. And while the first time around he agrees with what you have to say and seems to undergo the kind of enlightenment you have yourself experienced upon first hearing the theory you are presently relaying, within the month, or whenever you see him again, you find him repeating his previous lines, word for word, not suggesting that he has retrieved his old conviction by means of fresh reconsideration, but that he has altogether forgotten the conversation the two of you had originally had – I repeat: citing maxims on which refutation he had previously agreed. And as you wonder at his faulty memory, and so think it a good idea to repeat your previous line of reasoning, you discover that his memory was not in fact the problem; for as you begin saying the things to which he had previously listened, attentively and affirmatively, you see him wave them off, this time, with confidence that they can't be right or they do not interest him or he is beyond all that, and no discussion to the contrary can take place.

We may call this phenomenon an intellectual relapse. Those who read the Bible might call it a dog returning to his vomit (Prov. 26.11). The less eloquent among us would jot it down to stupidity. I think all three are correct in that they are more or less the same, the differences being in their salience rather than their diagnoses: for intellectual relapse is the failure to recognize stupidity, as is a dog's diet failure to understand the concept of vomit as a human would. Whatever your preferred expression, do note the complexity of the confusion, that being its two dimensions. The initial conversation revealed a misunderstanding of whim. The reason its resolution did not hold is misunderstanding of choice.

If you have not encountered this kind of person, I will ask you to indulge me: writing the example above, despite its generalized presentation, I had specific referents in mind, so I assure you that we are dealing with real-world phenomena. Moreover, it is not intellectual convictions alone that this lapse in judgment is known to affect, for which I also assure you that you have certainly met many people manifesting the two kinds of misunderstanding, in effect identical to the intellectual instantiation, but in practice a matter of behavior rather than propositional content. Keep in mind, the dog returning to his vomit is not about intellectual relapse, but spiritual relapse: not so much a stupid man failing to see stupidity as much as a foolish man (aren't we all) failing to recognize errancy. If you are a theist, you have no doubt seen many such instances (in yourself not least). If totally secular, then you have seen the same manifestation (in yourself not least) in secular fields of self-improvement, exercise, discipline, order, routine, mental health – you get the picture.

This is the paragraph on misunderstandings of whim. Intellectually, a whim is any belief you hold at a given moment. Conditioned as it is by the moment, it is liable to change for all kinds of reasons. You may hold firmly to the belief that taking a bribe is wrong, but you may also reconsider your position when exposed to the chance of actually profiting from a bribe, shrugging off your former conviction on a whim – as the whim that it has always been, the sudden influx of relativism or pragmatism that replaces it being also just another whim. We consider ourselves incorruptible (at least some of us), and though we may be factually incorruptible in fiscal regards, there are things for which we all potentially fall, be it material social or spiritual or somewhere in between; long-term or for a fleeting moment or just long enough for us to make the wrong decision. It is all whim, the beliefs we carry around, down to the particularities for which we stand. Friends who agree with you at one moment only to appear to have completely forgotten it all the next are prime examples of this – the favorable whim enabled by the setting, upon that initial conversation, allowed for open-mindedness, and the allure of whatever the opposite belief, lacking, for the moment, its usual pull, were the enablers of change – a good change, but not one without the possibility (or rather the guarantee) of reversal.

Given the chance and the circumstance, any whim can change into another. Yes, we are patriotic when we listen to the right kind of music, in the right setting we are militantly so, and in a sentimental mood we are sentimental; but change the music to a hymn to hedonism, and watch the tear-rending passion for one's country become a howl for wine women and song; a real-world war makes patriots turn pacifist, and good Christian sentiment goes out the window when our neighbor happens to annoy us – Ares is ever the preferable deity. There might be some readers preparing to voice disagreement with what I have just said – *this does nothing to change the fact that there is virtue in incorruption patriotism or sentiment or whatever!* and I agree, but what good is the virtue in sentiment patriotism or incorruption if it is a virtue that is present one moment and absent the next? Like a sentry sleeping on the job, it does not promise security against invaders; on the contrary, its sole promise is but an invader clever enough to sneak during snooze hours.

Cunning manipulators use this to the fullest; they can get a compliant nation shouting *freedom!* with a movie about courageous freedom fighters, only to turn this same audience tyrannous with a movie about a heroic military fighting a band of crazy rebels. They will get Christians to weep with joy at the sublimity that is our universal brotherhood in Christ, only to later threaten non-Christians to *GET OUT!* of the country they ruin with their reckless voting, those *godless vermin, hellbound and irredeemable through all of eternity, that scum of the Earth* they had just a little earlier accepted as the neighbors they are instructed to love. The manipulative prodigy will get hippies to hate conservatively minded people for their oppressive ways, and later sic these same hippies against oppressed people, acting in favor of the corporations that oppress them. Such is the mechanism of whim, and so dictates whoever controls it. It is for this reason that I do not care to address any misunderstandings of whim. Even if such a reader agreed with me on individual matters, he would change his mind just as easily given the circumstance. For coming to an agreement on any subject is, in such cases, also a mere agreement of whim, not choice; it is quasi-understanding.

On first glance, one might ask, *isn't choice a whim on its own?* Not quite. In our nomenclature, a choice is a conviction a person adopts as an intermediary between unconscious whim and conscious belief, between desire and action, or between impulse and decision.

It is meant to be a safeguard against the inconsistency of whim. In a sense, an intellectual choice can be made whimsically, however, that would not be much of a choice – just a whim parading as one. We can explain the two in an analogy presenting a dam and a river: the purpose of the former is to hold back the river; if the dam is in structure anything like the water behind it, it makes for a rather poor dam (and if it is entirely water, then it is not a dam at all). Yes, it is possible that even a good dam leaks from time to time, but the better the build-quality, the less this is likely to happen. I suppose another analogy would be that of a virtual private network: it protects some of the user's privacy, but this is far from protecting the user entirely – even his IP address might become vulnerable, though it is the only information the VPN is supposed to keep safe. Therefore, a good choice must not be whimsical in its origin, and, even when it does work as intended, it does not provide total security from whim – not without maintenance.

Some people make a choice that they ought to prioritize personal satisfaction. These are akin to people who have built their dams out of snow: its own essence is its contradiction. They have made no choice whatsoever but to lead a choiceless life, enslaved as they are to the flukes of whim. Then, there are those who make choices based on ideas not at all backed by the kind of theory needed to keep whim in line – supremacists of all kinds, most activists, ideologues in their teens, political analysts... an intellectual choice that is not intelligent will not prove a good choice in intellectual matters. At last, there are those who have based the choice that arbitrates their interpretations of personal whim on truth – on cold, hard reality as it is and as they see it (which is according to them one and the same), and they will always act, they believe, according to this reality – a truth, they hold, as objective as their adherence to it. They are the worst of the bunch.

Now, for the record, I am not a proponent of relativism – I do believe there is truth, and it is only one. Then again, did I not devote a good part of this chapter describing why our belief in it does not entitle us to its infallible recognition? Oh, I am one of those borderline fanatics who hold that films and books and songs have objective value – some are more valuable (objectively so), I believe, than others. But what of it? If I am too tired to enjoy a film, its value, objective or not, will be to me as that of a book I am too lazy to read or the factuality of a theory I cannot verify. What is the objectivity in good music, if it is the same as the objective fact of being in the right mood for it? Though I believe in an objective truth, how am I to know that I have the right angle on some particular question, when a morsel of information can turn political fanaticism into turncoat penitence and penitence will switch to turncoat fanaticism given the right headline?

People like to prove the fact of objective truth by saying that, in a bank, one cannot tell the banker that one has a million dollars in his bank account – because, objectively, he does not have a million dollars in his bank account. *And there you have it*, they say, *objective truth!* as idiotically as it befits them, never realizing that such things as money and your ownership of it and the power of banksters are such unreal constructs that their subjectivity compels their enforcement at gunpoint. If Napoleon issued a mandate that people of his stature are of above average height, and threatened dissenters with capital punishment, nobody would really believe that a 5'6" man is of above-average height, let alone use it as an example for the absoluteness of truth. Instead, we would whisper that the emperor has forced us to accept his own version of reality, which is in no way actual reality. So how comes it then that we accept the same myth, and we moreover consider it an excellent example of speaker-independent truth, when spoken by a banker – a creature far less impressive than Napoleon, mind you? Financial consensus is fine if regarded as a useful fiction in the establishment of financial order, but to use it as definitive evidence for the objectivity of truth is just silly.

Much of what we claim to know, we know only partially; most of what we think we ought to know, we misunderstand completely. That something is an objective fact tells us nothing particularly profound. To stick to the base facts we call objective is to skip the part that really matters. The tree outside, which I need to get cut lest it knocks down the roof during a windstorm, is not quite a tree – I have no reason to cut down a tree (I am rather fond of them); I have a reason to remove a problem. What is objectively a tree is in reality a problem – to me, that is to say, subjectively so. It is this idiomatic spin that relays the bit of information that is actually important. Then again, it is only a problem because it could *potentially* become a problem – as it stands, it is just a tree. It gives me shade and privacy alike. It is the opposite of a problem. So no, Mr. Reagan, although *a tree is a tree*, this tree is also a problem I need to address, but only potentially, and, factually, it is a convenience I would like to keep lush and fresh and green. To add to the confusion, once it has caused the problem we recognize as a damaged roof, the tree will once again become a tree, the problem having moved on to the damaged roof instead. Perhaps it is, as you might rightly point out, objectively, a *potential problem* I need to prevent from happening; but in that case it is also, just as objectively, a *factual blessing* I ought to keep – which I will not. Our infallible truth appears to contradict itself. Objective values only work at face-value, at which level they mean too little.

The thing is that facts, being the postulates of objective truth, cannot be so fuzzy as to block the possibility of essential knowledge. Therefore, to make *objective truth* one's intellectual choice is to have made no intellectual choice whatsoever – it is to put a very tall buoy in the middle of the river and call it a mighty dam. You will misunderstand the movie and find it objectively boring, you will disagree with the book's political message and think it objectively stupid; all fired up, you will look at the wrong news channel and objectively proclaim that it is the news channel that is wrong. At the same time, bigoted as you are, you will keep altering your beliefs at every whim in order to support a candidate or justify your theology or appeal to your superiors at work (or your ideology or idol or mentality), for your arbiter is not a truth you know, but a retelling of the world in compliance with your tastes. You will be at once fully surrendered to random whim, to whatever you happen to prefer at the moment (trained though your genre of preference may be, hence the illusion of impartiality), as is the man who has made the hedonistic choice, all the while remaining too enamored with the flattery that you are above it to realize what you have become. Instead of a person looking for objective truth, you are a functional lunatic generating a self-affirming dogma: the perennialism of your preferred whims.

Nevertheless, there is a solution. It is the alteration of choice from a choice of intellectual conviction into a choice of behavior – of action. Provided you make your arbiter of whim into an arbiter not of how you intellectually interpret whim, but of how you react to it, the tool on which you rely to make decisions will no longer be as fallible as the human brain. Instead, it will be the whole of your existence – inborn instincts, your natural senses (including empathy), bringing up, education, intelligence, and spirit. The only thing you need to do is word the following decision: my whims will be kept in line by the desire to do good.

The Universal Pederast

I will talk more about that in the next chapter. For now, let me tell you about the one kind of person with whom I would not talk – not even to explain to them the two kinds of misunderstandings. I am not being literarily dramatic. I really do refuse to converse with this kind of person – in real life, I have on many occasions removed myself from their presence (admittedly, not so boldly as to risk a charge of rudeness). I feel vindicated in disliking the archetype, for it is a man whose philosophy I consider beyond redemption: he is the man who justifies unambiguous manifestations of evil.

It is one thing to argue that an evil act was in reality morally gray: that a lowly criminal only stole to feed his family, that a high-class criminal was framed, or that evidence of atrocity has been misinterpreted; these range from stupid to abysmal to (rarely) reasonable, but they are not usually inexcusable as is the universal pederast. The reason I have given him such a repulsive name is no coincidence. It is not a retributive nickname that I have chosen for our villain, but a descriptive one.

People tend to agree on just how horrid a transgression it is to perform an act so gruesome that its very name I am trying to avoid mentioning directly, and so I only reference by implication. It is good that, no matter the discussion, this will always be a common ground for most people: the transgressor in such a case is a monster. It gives me hope that we may yet hold on to some fragment of a common morality, our other disagreements aside. What I would like to emphasize, now that we agree on a crime that, even according to the most tender-hearted, is all but unforgivable, is that the transgression we so abhor is not exclusively of the pederast's literal kin – it stretches farther, into a conceptually identical crime, and I am disgusted with this latter group for the same reason we are all disgusted with the non-metaphorical pederast.

It begins with the metaphor of predation. It is the one context in which people do not imagine the predator as a cool animal, and instead see him for what he is: a coward and a pest. Predators do not hunt game. They have no interest in strong animals; healthy adults of the species are a threat, not a meal. To the predator, it is the sick, the old, and the helplessly young that look the most appetizing. Predatory economy juxtaposes risk to reward, and it so happens that there is no profit like the kind proportional to weakness. And so, the most profitable are the most vulnerable. Predation is an insidious attraction checked by neither morality nor empathy nor honor – just an urge and little resistance.

It is the same with sexual predators. The cravings of one match the weaknesses of another. They do not look to win over somebody's heart with their own, nor do they look to compete over somebody's loins fairly; they only look for an easy meal. Prey is seldom imagined as a mighty elephant in his prime; prey is small and frightened. Prey is inexperienced. Prey is the most readily exploitable target. It is this theme that disgusts us the most when we hear about the crime. Of an adult man seducing, manipulating, or bullying a creature incapable to outwit outrun outkick or at all understand the threat it faces; a non-wolf with a wolfish mentality, and a lamb with human sensibilities. One ruined beyond repair, ruining another; one of them utterly guilty, the other so innocent it cannot even fathom such guilt. It is the worst crime a man can commit. Indeed, it is a crime so bad, that feminists will not mind me generalizing the perpetrator as male. Yet, I cannot avoid mentioning the less obvious side to this atrocity: it is merely an ornament.

You may focus solely on just how horrid it sounds, or you may escape the deception and understand the transgression for what it actually is. Sexual predation is but a subgenre of predation. It is the same motive we see in the sexual predator that we observe in any immorality committed in an exploitative dynamic: the mighty preying on the weak. The inexperienced, the innocent, the naïve; anyone who looks upon the world expecting goodness – these are the targets of crime, violent and nonviolent alike, legal and illegal immoralities, of coercion and solicitation, of scams and swindles; they are the demographic seen as prey by the demographic that likens itself to the predator. We see the latter all over: the boss who abuses his employees, the doctor manipulating his patients, the cop beating a suspect, the teacher who stomps on a student's dream, the parent who does the same, the overzealous critic, the scumbag running an online scam, the fire-and-brimstone preacher, the workplace schemer... these are no different that the molester we all agree we hate.

If you think their immorality is lesser because you do not see in their victims (their prey) the same overt vulnerability that you see in a child, then you are ignoring the concept for the sake of appearances. Keep in mind, there would be no exploitation if not for the vulnerable – for the needy, the naïve, and the weak – making for the predator an easy meal. The enthusiast trying to start a business, the dreaming artist, and the old person who does not understand the internet are no less vulnerable than children, and the perversity of the mind that would go ahead and hurt them is no different than its lecherous kinsman's. Genitalia is another ornament by the way. It tends to disgust people, and so, people fail to see the big picture. They assume that predatory economy is not as bad as predatory sexuality just because the former is not as gross. It is rather simple to prove that they are deceived: it is not the phallus of the sexual predator that is blamed, the sexual predator himself an innocent gentleman if not for that one rogue organ; it is the predator himself with whom we have an issue – his mentality, his indifference to his victim's suffering, his ability to either ignore (or else his inability to sense) any empathy or moral brake along any step of the way. No, the asexual nature of one predatory crime does not make it better than another. Neither should the appearance of the victims or what they mean to us affect our judgment, seeing as, in civilization, we are all equal – the outrage you feel at a particular crime cannot trivialize another, should your emotional reaction to the latter fail to live up to the standard of the former. Predators are evil without exception. They deserve equal judgment, for they are of the same perversion.

Understanding the transgression, that predation is the most heinous of individual crimes, consider next the kind of person willing to justify predatory behavior, and you will realize what kind of person I consider beyond repair (strictly intellectually), and my reasons for thinking so. What's more, in addition to defending them, the man who inspired this chapter has on occasion praised swindlers of this kind – he considers them smart, and their victims deserving of their fates – *it is your fault if you fall for it*, he said, *you are not entitled to protection from being stupid*. He thought himself brilliant for saying it, made all the more brilliant by the coldness in his voice, and I am sure that many would take his side if they heard him speak. I recognize it for a common disorder, as it affects many: the inability to first ask oneself if innocence really is tantamount to stupidity, then consider if the exploitation of innocence is itself not an infinitely worse intellectual error than any instance of naivety should be subject to the accusation; finally, to look at themselves and realize that, just as an aspiring musician could not tell a producer was shady, that just so are they themselves likely to fall for a scam in which they lack experience

– not restrained to social interactions, they do not realize that they are also potential prey to many deceptions (medical, political, any random business project, for instance); above all, they are not aware that they have fallen prey to greed that has consumed them thoroughly, being the spiritual predator that it is, and are lastingly swindled by shiny ornaments that have replaced their minds with the only stupidity a man *should* be faulted for practicing.

*

Being what he is, I have given up on the universal pederast. There is nothing I can tell him. I remember the first time I realized this, and I remember the relief I felt at it. It is one impossible fight less – another line to the battle hymn of the defeated, and with a rather soothing rhyme at that; if I am to wage an unwinnable war, I should at least make my defeat mean something. I did not pick up arms for just anything; I am doing this to prove a point, and a point ought to be proven only to those willing and able to appreciate proof.

Determining Undetermined Determining Meaning

With any option other than moral good, you are merely putting up a façade between whim and conscious decision, by which you either filter whim until it can effectively fool the system you call character, or you let it overwhelm you without even the pretense of self-control. To be morally good, Dear Reader, is the only choice you can truly call a personal choice, as it is the only way to ensure your independence from chance. If integrated properly, not only does moral good protect against intellectual relapse, but the proverbial dog's palate, in becoming educated against vomit, also becomes refined against many other humanly disgusting meals. I am not telling you that you will be forever good. All dams leak from time to time, which is why maintenance is important. Nor am I here to tell you when to stick to what is right and when to allow yourself the luxury of vice. I believe in my reader's best judgment on the matter. After all, we are trying to establish the means for consistency, not prevent all chance-deviation.

There is, of course, with what I propose, the problem of goodness, which is a fair contention to what I have said – what does it even mean to do good?! After all, I am asking people to integrate in themselves a subject so difficult to describe, and so subjected to personal interpretation, that many have been willing to proclaim the concept a non-reality on account of this challenge. Ironically, I do this shortly after having made an argument against the fallacy of adherence to an objectively accurate belief system. First, I tell you I cannot call a tree a tree, then I tell you I can call good *good*. But I regard the contradiction in that as an illusory conflict. None of us were born biologists. Nor have any of us been born trained semanticists. It should not surprise us that we have a hard time telling things apart, such as determining if a tree is in fact a problem, or that whales are not just enormous fish. But we have all been born human, and so we can tell right from wrong.[4]

We can all tell that taking something that does not belong to us is wrong, be it by education or empathy or both, that lying is bad, else it would not anger us, and that causing unnecessary suffering is evil, the person unable to realize this being labeled as mentally ill. Better yet, we can tell that making somebody else happy is good. Now, you could say that this is only because we have intellectualized our evolutionary pressure to uphold the community, i.e. the pressure not to exterminate our own species, and you would be free to believe that. I would not be surprised if it is a belief held by most people: *our moral sense is in reality just a Darwinian compulsion, existing for no other reason than to prolong our selfish genes.* I have no problem with that. But I thought we agreed that none of us was born a biologist. Even if our sense for right and wrong were just misinterpreted instinct, it is not an instinct we

---

[4] I do not count psychopaths and sociopaths for the same reason I do not count people born blind or deaf as arguments against human sight or hearing.

have any better chance of recognizing for an instinct than we have the chance to recognize good for good and bad as evil. The same goes for any observation regarding any factual state of affairs. We either trust our minds, or we do not.

Most refutations of the idea of goodness come from either a position of insufficient knowledge, or a position of insufficient consideration of knowledge. There is also a small selection originating from a position of pride. The entirety of the opposition against morality, however, unifying any and every such theory, stems from the common camp of an amoral intellectual choice. Whatever their ward against the malleability of the mind according to whim, it is not one intended for good. I have never met a man opposed to the idea of objective morality prioritizing matters of morality – in my experience, they tend to do the opposite, and so with *passionate intensity*. People who do live according to a moral system, however, tend to have no trouble telling apart right from wrong when it is time to act one way or another, even if they are intellectually unprepared to analyze either concept. It is practice that helps one tune their moral sensibilities, not theory – the same way that it is seeing that helps one attune to subjects of sight, not a degree in ophthalmology. But for the sake of argument, I will mention a few things to help people who have not given the subject much thought understand just how silly it is to judge morality a subject too dubious to consider true.

For the moral relativist, there is no need to despair. What I tell you is merely conceptual; it says nothing about reality as it is, but only about reality as we speak it. You may go on being morally relative if you so desire. My only goal at present is to establish the historic continuity of moral semantics – what you do with it is your business.

The most important thing to keep in mind is the disambiguation between $good_1$ and $good_2$. $Good_1$ is the morally neutral meaning of effective or preferable, as in a good car or a good ruler. $Good_2$ means moral goodness. This is entry-level polysemy: we can say that Caesar was a good emperor but a bad man, or that he was an effective ruler and also a bad ruler, or a good$_1$ ruler but not a good$_2$ ruler, and we would be allowed a chance of correctness in any propositional variation without danger of self-contradiction. I do not want anybody closing this book with the thought, *What is good for me may not be good for somebody else*, because that is among the least educated arguments to make – it is doubly as embarrassing when you hear a linguistics professor make it. Without even acknowledging good$_1$, the word has no meaning whatsoever. Then again, without accepting the distinct meaning of good$_2$, we would be able to make no difference between good men and bad men outside of a general claim on their effectiveness, i.e. an effective man and an ineffective man (or a preferable man and a not so preferable man), by which we get in a different kind of trouble: goodness has no distinct meaning outside its synonymy with the aforementioned concepts. This does not reflect reality as we know it, for as preferable as it must have been that the trains should run on time, and as effective a ruler as there was that made them so, most people will also agree that the person in question was by no means a good ruler, though he was an exceptionally good$_1$ ruler. Regardless, ignoring the crime against the lexicon, some insist that there is nothing wrong in good having no distinct meaning, as long as it supports their intellectual choice. But language will not allow it. Language exists to map the world; I explained this in my previous essay (37). It has the tendency, therefore, to change according to reality as we see it – to adapt to new cognitive environments, if you will, by which a word, even if limited in its conception, given the chance, becomes enriched with information on all dimensions perceptible to mankind. This makes semantic evolution somewhat of a linguistic law – no word can forever remain overly vague, nor can a concept have expressions counting unto redundancy. Therefore, even if a mere synonym to effective or preferable, the concept of good cannot have remained just that as mankind (mistakenly or otherwise) believed to have noticed a dimension so independent of effectiveness or the quality of being preferable, that, our ancestors believed, it must have been a distinct quality in need of linguistic determiners. This is how good$_2$ established its right to exist. Moral goodness is a linguistic necessity.

Our next step should be to determine whatever that means: to determine its determining meaning, even though, being as vague and as complex and as diverse a concept as it is, its determining meaning is from our perspective undetermined – meaning that we need to look for it if we are to have any chance of understanding it.

*

A common misconception regarding the difference between the exact sciences and those sciences that practitioners of the former regard as pseudoscience is the fallacy that it is exactitude that determines the validity of a science, in as far as an auxiliary fallacy stipulates that exactitude is to be ascribed exclusively to the kind of exactitude offered by the materially tangible. In reality, the only thing the status of natural exactitude secures is *security*. It is the security of measurement, to be precise, and, as such, the assurance of a safely derived conclusion. Moreover, it provides security to the recipient of knowledge: he needs not question what he learns, for an organelle granite and mass are all categories one can safely analyze for what they are; danger of error is solely in the measurement, not the thing itself.

Saul Bellow's protagonist in *Humboldt's Gift* kicks himself for being unable to understand the desires of people close to him; the only people other than himself, he observes, whose desires he knew were "non-existent people like Macbeth and Prospero" (405). Mister Citrine believes that this is because "the insight of language and genius" made the latter clear. I would here like to note that the language (or genius) to which he attributes his understanding is not of the characters, but of their creator. It is Shakespeare that is behind their clarity of expression. The exact sciences are oddly similar. Their concepts are predetermined. It is irrelevant, whether you call their determiner a conscious mind or blind chance. What matters is that subjects studied by physicists and biologists and geologists are settled externally. They are not their own creations, but the static expressions of a semantically consistent creator. The humanities, by contrast, can rely on no such convenience. The humanities are as if Macbeth were a real person, presently living, and in the position to refute whatever Mr. Citrine (or any other critic of the play) might have once assumed was his intention. Julius Caesar written by Shakespeare is a much safer Caesar than Julius Caesar sans script. Nor is it a coincidence that even though Shakespeare's characters have been thoroughly studied and (we believe) understood, we cannot tell much concerning Shakespeare himself. The human element disallows such boldness as could enable definite conclusions.

No matter how sound a humanist's argument, his theory is like a gladiator in the ring: it is meant to be attacked, attacked at its weakest point, antagonized by government opponent and subject alike, and often overruled not by a stronger fighter but by a louder crowd; in such instances, he is unable to do anything to decisively prove himself right – he has no rock, on occasion literally, on which to make his stand. It is no wonder that cowardly humanists have retreated to the safe haven of statistics – those cannot be disproven, even if Macbeth were to publically disagree with them – *No, Mr. Macbeth, it does not matter if you were arrogant ambitious gullible insecure or evil or impressionable; the data we've gathered on your socioeconomic impact through income tax revenue in small and medium-sized enterprises in medieval Scotland is unmistakable!*

Whatever a humanist wills to research, he will first need to carve into a precise semantic mold; he cannot do this but by thorough semantic experimentation. We do not have the luxury of external measurement – of anything determining our subject for us. The reason the humanities do not have the honor of being called *exact* sciences is not for a comparable lack of thinking, but the opposite.

I told you this in order to get the naturalistic prejudice out of the way before attempting what I tell you next: moral good is a clear, valid concept, in theory and in practice alike. This is a demonstrable truth. I will demonstrate it by rooting our knowledge of moral goodness in a fact in which every other fact is rooted also. The fact of which I speak is the fact of human cognition, namely the belief that it is valid. Our definition will be epistemologically stable, and doubly as humane.

*

Emergent properties, or modern moral values, should be simple to determine, seeing as they are values with which most people will not disagree. Let us consider: determination, fairness, kindness, tolerance, compassion, open-mindedness, honesty, having a healthy work ethic... Are these attributes likely to be greeted with disagreement, i.e. should we expect anyone to argue in favor of being a quitter, unfair, rude, bigoted, sociopathic, stubborn, a liar, or lazy – and not so in the sense that he would prefer to practice the latter for being easier, but because he honestly believes them to be morally good, i.e. morally superior to their opposites? If there is anyone who disagrees that fairness, kindness, compassion (etc.) are good, it is not because he disagrees with these specific manifestations of moral goodness, but because he disagrees that there is such a thing as moral goodness altogether. Clearly, whatever debate may arise on the question of *what does it mean to be good* is not a debate that can cast doubt on the kind of character and virtues we consider good. We all know this, moral nonrealism notwithstanding. If we are to trust our cognition, if we are to call it valid, if we mean to consider ourselves capable of knowledge and of learning, we must draw a conceptual line somewhere: a lazy sociopath yelling at people while slacking at work cannot be morally good. The burden of proof is not on me to show that the values I have mentioned above are regarded as moral values in the modern world – on the contrary: the burden of proof is on the skeptic to prove that they are not. This goes for any individual virtue or set of virtues we can think of – if they cannot be expected to come up to opposition, or if their opposites are not regarded as morally superior, then they are moral values of the emergent world.

30

But not restrained to their modern iterations, there is an observable continuity in these virtues we can trace as far back as the Middle Ages. Arguably before that, although it is hard to tell how well-established they might have been when they first appeared in spoken form. To choose a neutral and non-doctrinal source, as neutral and as non-doctrinal as we can find among our medieval ancestors, let us consider the Sermon on the Mount: blessed are the poor (5.3), those who weep (5.4), the meek (5.5), those who hunger and thirst after righteousness (5.6), the merciful (5.7), those with pure intentions (5.8), the peacemakers (5.9), and those who face persecution for their faith (5.10). We may sum these up as modesty, compassion, tolerance, love of justice, tender-heartedness, honesty, and fortitude. In that sense, there is perfect compatibility with the modern iteration of morality, seeing as tolerance, compassion, honesty, and righteousness (fairness) appear in the modern virtues I have listed, as well as an assumed connection with virtues I have not listed, considering modesty and fortitude would not be contended or argued as morally inferior to greed and cowardice. If the religious nature of the source makes you biased, either for or against it, then consider Shelley's comment that, a man, "to be greatly good, must imagine intensely and comprehensively; he must put himself in the place of another and of many others; the pains and pleasures of his species must become his own." It sounds quite compatible with the old system and the new, despite the fact that it was written by a poet of the so-called *Satanic School*.

We have thus observed a consistent moral standard through centuries of ethical tradition, and so, what we value today is certainly not purely contemporary or even significantly different from what people considered righteous in the Middle Ages. If anything, whatever change has come about, our conception of justice has improved parallel to our understanding of the old values, as we have amplified meekness (or tolerance), we have put an end to slavery for we are compassionate, and we no longer look up to the rich and powerful as gods, for we have learned to appreciate modesty.

Furthermore, a similar conceptual lineage can be traced all the way back to the esteemed cradle of civilization, i.e. to ancient thought, whereby the Classical Virtues, which are said to have been virtues commonly praised by philosophers, are courage, justice, moderation, and wisdom – all of them compatible with the moral system of the pre-modern and the modern era alike. Indeed, there are some points of conflict, such as, for example, the fact that meekness may not have been looked upon as necessarily noble in the ancient world, and, in the modern world, ambition and self-determination tend to play a larger role compared to modesty, however, that is mostly a question of development – first of mutation, i.e. deviation, and then, depending on its success, either evolution or retardation.

And there we have it. It is possible to synthetize a functional meaning of moral good that is at the same time reflective of linguistic tradition and the linguistic reality of the present. We did not even need to rely on lists of citations or on thousands of pages of ethical theory. We only assumed that we are capable of forming a functional picture of reality, and we posed but two questions: what do we value now, and what did our ancestors use to value then? The answer allows for an eclectic definition of morality as an amalgam of set virtues, and it demonstrates the conceptual existence of such a thing as $good_2$.

*

The only other thing to consider is how these relate to the practice I proposed at the beginning of this chapter: how does this definition work with choosing goodness as an arbiter between whim and action? The answer is to keep in mind, when making a moral decision, the congruence of your actions with a set of virtues which practice does not lead to a kind of scrutiny such that the practice of the opposite is posited as the morally superior practice;

and, to ward off against potential mutations arising on either side, to consider if what you do is compatible with modesty, tolerance, righteousness, compassion, and courage, as a base set of moral qualities, and let us add sincerity for assurance. However you view these qualities (virtues or delusions or just some elusive urges), the fact remains that, if most people (or at least a good majority of people) practiced them, i.e. they truly agreed on them, there would be far less cases of chronic misunderstanding in the world.

Going back to the analogy of the dam, anything else is a gateway to either excuse a preferable leak or else refuse to acknowledge the flood as a problem altogether. Therefore, if you decide to establish the will to do good as the barrier between whim and action, you will have accomplished something that many do not: you will have made the only decision that stands a chance against the chaos of unbridled whim and the perils of ineffectively guarding against it.

A Rule of Dumb

You can tell a lot about the things people value by how they brag about their kids. It is by no means the definitive statement on social capital, but whatever they feel comfortable sharing and whatever they feel obliged to lie about are good indicators of the moral framework arbitrating the conversation. By moral framework I mean the understanding that there is such a thing that determines *should* from *should not*, and aligns, according to these, qualities and achievements along a scale of positive comparative and superlative, and, on the opposite end, the negative that is most frequently left out. I had the pleasure of witnessing such a demonstration not too long ago, and it was an event that annoyed me intellectually to the same extent that it left me emotionally indifferent, seeing as, despite its offense to the intellectual faculty, I have grown used to hearing others like it, reiterated among people of similar standing, and, now with the wisdom of experience, have learned better than to react to them, either emotionally or conversationally. In retrospect, my silence at the time turns out to have been an idea much wiser than base diplomacy, for recollecting the event has given me something to write about. It was only by an open mind (and clenched teeth) that I figured out the content you are about to read in this chapter, and all that from what was otherwise a fleeting instance of barbershop small talk.

The setting is clear from the previous sentence. I was getting a trim, as the man next in line was talking about his son. The first thing he said was that his son is six feet and seven and a half inches tall. Out of all the virtues unique to mankind, the proud parent's first boast was of his son's likeness to a giraffe. The next thing he said was that his son travels a lot and goes out with girls even more, the latter being a quick, almost dismissive comment, as if not meant to be accentuated, disregarding the fact that its evocation was by itself accentuation. Of course, it is men who complain the loudest about *those perverts* in parliament or churches or schools that are also first to encourage their own children into promiscuity. At last, he said that his son was not at all interested in school, but that he had a good mind for business – *for business*, he said, *he is very good*. I never learned what that is supposed to mean. If it refers to the kid being able to consistently get a job done, then I assume the proud parent would have said so; the same goes for the qualities of being a hard worker or an honest tradesman. As it stands, a mind for business is either a meaningless phrase or a euphemism for business antonymous to mending the law. Up to this point, it is the usual braggart twaddle, total deception by ornament and neglect of language; but it was what came after that makes up *the plot* of this chapter.

They went on to talk about how school is pointless – how useless the things they teach, never to be used in real life, how outdated the model of learning and studying and testing knowledge has become, how easily pupils can now outwit their teachers (in the sense that they cheat on tests), and just how inane education really was for them as well – the grownups, you see, who spent so much time studying and all for nothing!

Now, Dear Reader, I can understand the bragging in the previous paragraph – I do not approve of it, but I believe we ought to tolerate it. If there is one thing that even the least perceptive parent could notice in their kid, it is their change in stature; it is arguably the safest quality of which to boast. The approval of the opposite gender, moreover, is such a valued indicator of social status that it can excuse all the deadly sins plus insincerity if they can be proven to have been committed in the name of securing a confirmed bodycount. At last, a good mind for business is among the politest ways of saying a mind good for nothing in particular. No, whichever part of that paragraph I find annoying, I must forgive. But I would be sinning against intellect to allow an attack on education go unaddressed. Because this was not a revolt against a lack of education, as intelligent people criticize the institution, i.e. against teachers not teaching, against students not being allowed to learn, against nobody getting smarter – the dumbing down of the school system, if you will; this was the opposite – the speaker in question was echoing the creed of the simpleton-rebellion, namely he was complaining that teachers teach students, that students are made to learn, and that they are not allowed to remain stupid! Our upstanding citizen was not a man complaining about a lack of quality, but a man looking to uproot the very possibility of quality. It was an anti-intellectual sentiment, and, I must add, the sentiment that is the reason our education system has become so dull and dulling: people don't want it to get good.

*

I was in high school when I realized I wanted to be a writer. I did not become one then and there (it would be a while before I wrote anything resembling a completed piece of fiction), but it was around that time that I felt the urge to make literature the main objective of my career. You may find it surprising, then, that I did not really like literature class. Not at first. Though I wanted to write and I obviously acquired this desire by reading, I had no interest in reading (or writing about) Voltaire and Moliere and Balzac and Dostoyevsky and Tolstoy and (as surprising as it seems now) Shakespeare. I considered Jane Austen the height of pretense. Regardless, I developed a sincere liking for literature class despite the fact that I did not develop any interest in Dickens or

Beckett or Goethe at the time. It began as curiosity for what is valued in literature, but it did not prove especially productive in that sense. Rather, it was a social and (arguably) spiritual drive that motivated my change of preference. If I first approached the subject for writing-tips, which, it matters that I stress, I did not get, I came to enjoy it in the long run for its ambient, which I got to experience in abundance. Discussing themes and motifs and characters proved a rewarding experience in many ways. So much so that I looked forward to it, the way I normally looked forward to recess, and I have no memory of being bored or wishing to skip this class in particular, as it really did not feel like class at all, but a pleasant break from schoolwork. My friends considered this new development unusual.

Our Literature professor had a fearsome reputation. No students (even the delinquents) dared talk without permission. On an eventless day, you could hear the dust settle. During a quiz, you could just about hear teeth chatter. But this apparent strictness changed whenever a student worded his or her opinion on a piece. Our otherwise strict professor became a lively, talkative woman, interested in hearing what others think, careful to correct them if they erred too badly, and willing to go an extra mile to check if an interpretation held up – with a surprisingly liberal standard at that. The silence in the classroom turned into lively conversation.

Now, for the record, this is not a story of charity – of a disinterested pupil being nice to his teacher to make her happy; on the contrary: our professor was a well-off woman with a family – she was very clearly happy outside the classroom, as she was content enough that there should be discipline in it. Our enjoyment was optional. Please, do not misinterpret this as a grumpy-to-happy story arc. No, she did not turn into a bubbly cartoon-character at the sound of a pupil's voice. Rather, the change in her had the air of a person who enjoys their work – a person passionate about a subject encountering people who enjoy the same things that she does; a person who believes that her professional purpose is nobler than awaiting the next paycheck, having received proof that her work is indeed nobler than her timely paycheck. When there was discussion, the cold, authoritarian atmosphere went from a variety of dull bordering on oppressive to pleasant bordering on nothing other than the immediate pleasantness of the scene. At least for those of us who participated. The others (possibly the majority) generally hid behind their monitors hoping to avert her gaze. I am sure the roles were partly reversed during math class, provided, unlikely though it is, that math-nerds have souls, and that math teachers will not have consumed them (their souls) for sustenance. It is an interesting dynamic either way, that pleasure and boredom can exist at the same place and at the same time.

I contacted this professor a while ago to let her know I am now a published writer, and the experience, in our current jargon, was what we describe as wholesome. I was happy to hear that the project-presentation I had made on Kafka (fully-illustrated, as is my standard), is a presentation she shows her students to this day. We reminisced about much, all good, and with good reason – there was enjoyment to be shared – then as well as now. It was the same for many other teachers and many other subjects. They all wanted to see their students engaged in class. Our Logics teacher, for instance, did turn into a bubbly cartoon-character when students were willing to debate him – even when I was vocally opposed to his spirituality; Sociology, Law, Music – all classes that most of my peers would consider useless, and all of them classes to which some of us looked forward on account of this reciprocity between student and students and students and teacher.

I stress: this is not about fake interest or simply making the teacher's day. I despise people who do that. Insincere interest is one of the worst offenses of our time. The interaction I have recorded describes curiosity developing into genuine investment – a real interest that only grew in intensity; not an illusion that only grew in deception. The moral of this story could not be real if our interest was not real as well. But the moral itself does not have pleasure for its end – at least not in its fully actualized form.

For what it's worth, I do think I have gained valuable knowledge in these classes. Although Tolstoy may not have taught me anything at that age, I believe I have learned many things from his prose between then and now. Although I considered Karl Marx and Max Weber useless at the time (albeit interesting), my knowledge of them, basic as it was, allowed me to look upon society from angles I could not have even considered without their theory. Only a total ignoramus (the totality here refers to his pride) would confidently proclaim that school has taught him nothing, or that it was useless because he had forgotten everything in the meantime – as if failure to apply knowledge is a sign of anybody's stupidity other than the man guilty of the failure; or as if him leading such an intellectually dull life that he forgot all that he used to know is somehow the fault of the people who once taught it to him.

The moral, however, is that irrespective of what they taught me, i.e. even if I stood to gain nothing from these classes – even if they were as thoroughly pointless as a proud ignoramus wishes to convince himself they must have been, and there was no valuable knowledge to gain from learning about Chekhov and Byron – the act of participating in class, of studying the subject matter and interacting with my professors and my classmates, was in itself an act that shaped us in ways so essential to the proper development of young persons, that no other institution has the ability to train as effectively or as intensely. This is so because schoolwork is the one remaining formal rite of passage. It ticks all the marks. It is handed down from one generation to another – the institution as well as the knowledge gained. Those who pass become forever altered as mature adults. It is a feat that, to the young and unwise, seems pointless and weird. It is a thing that the uncivilized view with contempt. It is an act of self-sacrifice for the community – of giving up a part of one's own free time, denying oneself the privilege of leisure to make one's teacher and one's classmates, in essence one's own people, experience something nice at some point in their day. None of this is overly poetic. They are perfectly literal things students do. To add a private joke in a class-presentation is to think of others. To make it tasteful is to begin to mature. To add one's sincere opinion to an essay is an attempt to save the world. To word it intelligently is to think like a philosopher. To study for a test is to test your trust in your ancestral legacy. To try to get a good grade is to take care of your parents. To do well in school is to answer the call of all men, which is to stand for reason, to do for others, to build communities and maintain societies and to oppose the most potent antagonist to one's manhood: one's own version of one's self – the selfish, the lazy, the hedonistic, the pigheaded, the boyish. School, at its most effective, teaches; at its dullest, it matures. Of all the people that I know from either high school or college, the only decent people are those who gave it an honest try – who worked hard to do well, even if not all of them succeeded at it. The descendants of the proud ignoramus, who knew from the get-go that school is pointless, they proved an invariably pigheaded, boyish, hedonistic, lazy, selfish breed into adulthood; they have not worked to form (nor uphold) any communities, and their accomplishments fail to impress; they are capable of no feats of self-denial in the name of anything, and reason is rather low on their list of priorities. Those who took school seriously, however, are people with whom I keep in touch to this day; not all of them are successful, but they are good people.

I do not pretend that this is true in all cases. I have personally known many straight-A students who were insufferable, and who remain insufferable in the present. Theirs was the wrong kind of schoolwork. Their ambitions had nothing to do with building a community or self-denial or having a good time in class – if they studied, they studied because that was all they could do; if they appeared to deny themselves with perfect effectiveness, it was because they had no such thing as a self to struggle denying, and their interactions with the teachers were not about pleasure but sycophancy. I have also known teachers who preferred an oppressive atmosphere to a good class – who created and maintained unease, who played favorites, who saw the grading system as a power-trip. These are people who do not see their job for the responsibility that it is. Such people are why even good students tend to slack in some subjects.

Yet, is that the school system against which the proud ignoramus rants? Is that the system he wishes to see changed for the better? Not at all! And that is my point. You will not hear the braggart ignoramus accuse the education system when it fails to be effective. On the contrary: when the education system is a mockery of what it used to be, he praises it! This man is happy that his son can cheat on tests, or that teachers give him good grades in spite of his failure to learn; when a good kid performs poorly, he is ecstatic – *all the more reason to hate schooling!* and the same goes when a bad kid does well. It is only when a teacher happens to demand that students understand the subject matter, that our ignoramus protests: *what is this useless bull?! We didn't need it then and my kids don't need it now either!*

Ironically, it is the most ardent critic of the education system that is the reason the education system deserves criticism in the first place: he undermines it, hoping to see it uprooted. As I said earlier in this chapter: the rage against teachers is not rage against bad teachers – it is rage against good teachers; their defective colleagues are just a pretext for the attack. All along, it has been but one campaign against effective schooling, in an ongoing war against intellect and intellectuals.

*

I speak of education as a thing of great importance. I stand by it. I also see the apparent irony in citing from Diogenes Laertius a little earlier, the same source who notes that Aristotle regarded education as "an *ornament* in prosperity and a refuge in adversity," (emphasis added) shortly after criticizing the masses for their deception by ornament. But do keep in mind that, in this life, we are at all times exposed to adversity. Education, as such, makes up the battlements of understanding, not a decorative piece above the fireplace. Besides, even if it is an ornament, under ideal conditions, it is an ornament akin to the hide of the Nemean lion – a practical trophy, offering the protection it does, and being permanent as it is – this is by Aristotle's own admission.[5]

Which is not to say that people are not deceived with it. What else do you think is the obsession with long lists of cited works and peer-reviews? Prestigious universities? Why do you think it matters to the lot? The modern intellectual's obsession with cited content over quality of argument is an annoyance I have addressed (in prose) at least twice before. To briefly do it again: it should not be to the detriment of my hypothesis if I say something that, being an idea with which I have come up on my own and have independently formed into a theory, has not been previously said by somebody else – it is a travesty, I reckon, that originality is greeted not with inquiry but with anathema. I find it all the more absurd when a theory to which one has come just as independently, and presents it in just as unique a manner, is discredited not for being wrong, but for a version of it, or rather an iteration resembling it, having been said elsewhere before. We observe two separate and opposite scenarios leading to the same marginalizing outcome: if it has not been said before, it must not be relevant; if it has been already said, then it is irrelevant.

Which illogic, together with the practical impossibility of its circumvention, sketch, in my view, the inkling of ornament. As if the thousands of papers being published all around the world are easy to access, free of charge, and so well-organized that a person can, in the abundance of the free time we have, in addition to the energy we possess in equal proportion, study them diligently, from the first historical instance of an argument, to the latest commentary on its relevance, and so in every segment on which its veracity depends, and with just as many tangents many times over, just so we can make a statement regarding something we already know. One gets the impression that it takes a tome to write

---

[5] "Education he declared to be the best provision for old age" (Laertius).

a paragraph, and a miracle to state an original opinion. This standard, by the way, is something that the academicians upholding it fail to meet themselves, even though they are paid to get it right – their research, even when packed with citations, is embarrassingly lacking in what should be essential theory. Which is how I know the inkling of ornament has led us to the ornament-proper: the external assurance of quality, regardless of the "damnèd error," when some snobbish brow will "bless it and approve it" with a peer-review, "hiding the grossness with fair ornament."[6]

Having published seven books, and having one book published for me, I can tell you two things: first, it is the latter over which I have *bragging rights* among intellectuals – they are impressed that somebody wanted to publish *my* book, and so they congratulate me on my success, though I merely wrote the manuscript, sent it to the publisher, and waited until it went public. The other thing I mean to tell you is that I regard my seven self-published books with greater sentiment: I wrote them; I edited, proofread, and formatted each text; I designed every cover, I made them fit, and I promoted the books on my own. The former is a kid I sent to a boarding school, the latter I saw through adulthood. But regardless of my personal experience with publishing, I generally do not talk about them. People need the assurance of authority to let them know that something is good, whereas self-published content has only the assurance of the self. It demands the same judgment in its estimation. Only *you* can attest to its quality. I understand some people find this a suboptimal requirement. It is no wonder, therefore, that they chase after trend and critics and ornament of similar significance. You will, in consequence, hear about *the most influential* and *the most relevant* or *the most popular* in regards to any sold product – intellectual products especially. But in spite of such superlatives reserved for content that ought to be regarded as the best, you will not hear any of it described as *the best*.

---

[6] This is from the same speech in *The Merchant of Venice*.

That is actually the good angle to the swindle: it means that those of us willing to think for ourselves have no competition – well, no competition that is any *good*. Because, whereas we cannot speak of historical writers as *the best* because we are yet to compare all that they have done to all that will be done, a lot of it under their influence, and so we avoid referring to them as the best, the reason that modern figures in literature are described as *influential* or *popular* or *esteemed* is for the fact that their promoters are aware that these pawns will never be *the best*. They are not even good – else, they would have called them that. Keep in mind, though we cannot with certainty call Dickens the best English novelist of his time, we can without a doubt call him a good English novelist – and not just for his time, mind you. This epithet is not reserved for modern-influential-popular-esteemed-relevant creators of content – neither artistic nor academic. Good literature is yet to become the best literature, while mediocre literature is permanently well-reviewed.

With that, having observed the deception in detail, I would not call education an ornament – at least not in the sense of a *deceptive* ornament. When it deceives, it is not really education. How could we call it education, when education leads to understanding, to a betterment of the rational faculty, but its ornamental perversion manifests as a degradation of the ability to think for oneself – as overdependence on canonized intellect over reliance on one's own competence? It is not education, but validation that parades around what we call modern academia. From there, I conclude that education can be a deceptive ornament only when it is not itself, namely when something has taken on its outward appearance, but has really nothing to do with either knowledge or rites of passage. A diploma is only as good as the name written on it, or the character for which the latter stands; merely hanging on the wall, it is but a talentless attempt at decoration.

Nor should we neglect, for that reason, that the opposite (lack of education) is also an ornament – a commodity that some people think looks nice, and with which they are willing to boast. While there is no accounting for taste, and so, I would not normally judge it, it is a preference for annihilation – the extermination of an institution and those in it – which rebuke on my end is vindicated as self-defense. Notice how our subject for the chapter described his son as superior to his teachers, and so not because the kid knew more than his teachers, but because he knew less. We are at a point in time when hatred of the intellectual has reached such an extreme level, that it is stupidity that has taken on the form of a virtue, and it is knowledge that is a silly little deviance – a regressive thing, even.

*

It is not a pleasant observation to make. It is quite the shock to witness how the propensity to think is met with negative reaction. When we are in the position to share our knowledge, i.e. when another is obliged to listen, we are met with scorn; when we are not in the position to share our knowledge, or when nobody is forced to listen, we are met with mockery. Even among the learned, there is not a shared desire for learning, but an assumed hierarchy, subcommunicated pride in being ignorant of other sciences – the belief that a learned man ought not to learn further: a doctor does not need to know your philosophy, for a doctor is smarter than a philosopher; a philosopher does not care about art because he is a man of thought and art is sentimental humdrum; nor does an artist care for the everyman's craft because craft is too lowbrow and dirty and sweaty a thing for the upper-class beatnik. Likewise, the everyman does not seem interested in anything, for he knows that neither philosophy nor art will get him ahead – though, I should note, he makes an exception for the doctor, to whom he believes it is prudent to suck up. Artificial intelligence is already being promoted as a suitable substitute for education, almost immediately after it was accepted as the thing to put an end to art. The fact that it is this type of advertisement that people find appealing is all the more proof of the anti-intellectual trend. Earlier technology has made a similar attempt, and with no small success at that – a calculator a dictionary a map a translator a painter a musician and all kinds of facts stored in a man's pocket for whenever he needs them, topped off with distractions like social media and entertainment and mind-numbing games on the same device to ensure that he has minimal need for these substitutes for the bettering of the mind of which he has little use to begin with. In the ongoing evolutionary development of mankind, the following prediction gains in probability, that the next trait to go will be the mind – our defining quality is headed the way of fur.

I think it has to do with another contemporary fallacy, which has to do with a pseudoscientific take on evolution, itself related to a certain phobia hidden beneath just enough layers of bravado to remain undetected. People who do not think much tend to think too much of Darwinism. I blame the curriculum. Ask anyone about the difference between the Roman Empire and the Roman Republic, the signing of the Magna Carta, or the conclusion of the French Revolution, and you will find that they know very little if anything about these events (this is not their fault by the way). But ask them about the origin of man, and you will hear the same answer or a variation thereby: *Ook! Ook! Eek! Eek!* – in varying levels of eloquence. That point in history has been proclaimed too essential a lesson in western culture. Between the Second World War, The American Revolution, the rise of Rome, the fall of Rome, the establishing of Christendom (also within Rome), chief relevance in modern historiography is relegated to Darwin's histories.

It is important to stress that event as historical – the timeless instance when man began to walk upright, to think upright, and to consider *ape* an insult. I am told that history matters because it tells us who we are. Now I notice that, while nobody gives a damn about their ancestors of antiquity or the Middle Ages or the pre-modern era (I personally know people who do not know the names of their own great-grandparents), allegedly because they cannot relate to any of them, they yet look for their roots at an instance that is almost entirely speculative and biologically impossible to relate to

– they think of themselves as the descendants of apes. Modern man looks for who he is within a creature he is certainly not.

As I speculate there will at some point be, in my accidental audience, the kind of person who imagines himself growing smarter with each reiteration of his belief in Darwinian evolution, let me briefly note that I am not actually criticizing the theory of evolution itself. I am talking exclusively about the emphasis that is given to it in education, and its mythical expansion into effective totemism. It is impossible for a man to be closer to an ape than it is for him to be closer to his human ancestors – *especially* in terms of biology. In spite of this, however, I notice people accepting a non-rational creature as their closest relative, while ignoring millennia worth of their true ancestry as something too distant to matter. That is all there is to my argument. I have nothing against Darwin himself – I would not have painted him on the front cover otherwise.

Moving on, I assume the anomaly I describe might have to do with a willingness on the part of some people to be just as non-rational as the creature they look to adopt as their ancestor, but I would not speculate on it just yet. The absurdity in question has not been a fact for long. Whatever its cause, it must be recent. And *that* is what I want to discuss next.

*

Now, make no mistake, I do not deny the appeal of sexuality. It has been a rather prominent motif throughout history. But whereas studying renaissance culture teaches us that Shakespeare wrote the occasional dirty joke, modern culture tries to teach us that it is *all* a dirty joke – art, culture, history, legacy, love, religion, our very lives are but a long, flopping charade. But you do not read Hamlet's reference to homosexuality (2.2 332-335), and on account of laughing at it ignore the preceding lines on the meaning of life, or the poeticism with which he words them. The only person capable of such a blunder is the Freudian literary analyst, as he struggles to reconcile a story about fathers and sons, indecision, and all-round skepticism, into a longwinded ode to incest.[7] The allusion to oral sex in *The Taming of the Shrew* (2.1 222-232) is not appreciated because of the allusion, but because of the pun – it is wittily crafted and competently executed; it is a tongue-in-cheek (no pun intended) instance in an overall stellar comedy; it is not at all like the modern take on adult humor, which is a brazen filibuster in cheap farce.

People in the renaissance understood something about sexuality that we do not – nor are we likely to understand it, irrespective of the national budget on Sex ed. Consider Christopher Marlowe, a known lecher (albeit with accusations from unreliable sources), when he makes a dirty joke regarding two demons, male and female, whereby the male demon has horns, and the female "clifts and cloven feet" (4. 94-97). This is how a peasant describes the creatures. Now, contrast it to Faustus himself, the overeducated protagonist, reacting to his first acquaintance with a demon: "Thou art too ugly to attend on me!", and he demands that Mephistopheles return in the form of "an old Franciscan friar," because "That holy shape becomes a devil, best" (3. 30-32). The peasant guffaws at sexual innuendo. The nobleman chuckles

---

[7] This is a real thing, and a very popular interpretation. From what I know, the theory begins with one Ernest Jones in 1910, who argued that Hamlet's behavior is explicable by the Freudian theory of repressed incestuous desire. Jones interprets such things as Hamlet's hesitation to kill the king as indicative of ulterior motives not related to vengeance. Coming from a long lineage of master-assassins, I can see why Jones thought regicide an easy task, though it cannot have been as easy for Hamlet, untrained as he was in the art. Jones also believes that Hamlet's frustration with his mother for remarrying is a sign that Hamlet wanted her for himself (sexually) – and here I concur, there is no other possible explanation for Hamlet's feelings. Jones emphasizes the scene where Hamlet throws his mother on the bed in anger as clear evidence of sexual desire. I can forgive him the hasty conclusion, as he probably did not know that the original text had Hamlet throwing the old woman on the floor, but her stunt-double's insurance did not cover broken bones, as per Renaissance workplace safety law.

politically. There was a hierarchy, at the time, which put temperance on one end, and indulgence on the other; one was cleanliness, the other filth; one exalted, the other lowly. We were meant to strive for the former. But now, it is the Falstaffs of the world who make the rules. It is people interested in nothing unless it were "a fair hot wench in flame-coloured taffeta" (King Henry 1.3) that coin the canon on what ought to interest us. On this note, I was going to say that the shift in balance happened as peasants were allowed to think like noblemen, but I have thought better of it. It cannot be that free education is to blame – did not time-travelling Chesterton tell us that a good thing is always good, and a bad thing always bad? No, I cannot agree with the elitist (not even on this account); education is good, and it is best that as many people are permitted it as will have it. The true cause for the deviation is best worded as the following alteration of my initial proposition: it is not that the descendants of peasants try to think as noblemen, but that noblemen have come to think like peasants.

The answer came to me one afternoon as I was listening to the song of the birds in a non-proverbial bush – creatures of which I have always been fond, and creatures regarding which sound I was surprised to hear people's tastes are divided. The half of us who do enjoy avian melodies agree that nature's chirps whistles and chitters produce a soothing sound, never minding its context. It was in regards to this that one thusly awoken person made an online comic about people enjoying as music what is in reality an ongoing shout for mating – what to our ears sounds like singing, to the birds themselves, the illustrator argued, is just a continuous iteration of copulation-requests. This is wrong – even biologically. But the comic got enough traction to become somewhat of a viral phenomenon, which popularity is proof that many people believe that such is indeed the case. It is not just the comic, mind you – wildlife documentaries tend to overemphasize the urge to mate as well. As I remembered it just then, I thought how, in antiquity, the backward-minded pagan would think to himself that birds exist to produce beauty, and, if they needed the incentive of copulation to do so, it was only because they lacked the intelligence to create beautiful things for their own sake; I thought how, in the Middle Ages, an illiterate peasant would think to himself that birds are similar to man because they also sing, however, man does not need the incentive of immediate pleasure to sing, because the beauty of which man is capable is above the scope of the worldly. I contrasted this to the modern educated man, who, upon observing a creature that is not of his species, does not only fail to see the profound difference between it and himself, but doubles his crime against perception by likening not the lower creature to himself, but himself to the lower creature. To make his idiocy perfect, he comes to identify with it: he hears birds singing and he thinks that it is because of sex, and this must mean that it is all about sex, and that he must therefore be all about sex as well. *Beauty*, he concludes, *is just horny for uneducated people.*

I meet truck drivers to this day, who believe they have the authorship rights to whatever comes out of the factory – *I made it!* they proudly say, *it is mine!* even though they do not own the factory nor do they have any idea how the thing is actually made. They do not even know what to do with it once it has come out. The truth is that nobody has authorship rights in this regard – not even the factory manager herself, for she is neither an inventor nor a worker – she merely owns the structure – and yet, she too, in her ignorance, considers herself the owner and creator of the product. This is yet another side-effect of the overemphasis we place on the biology lesson we ignore beyond the dirty part. Children will be better off once we've realized what an absurdity it is – how horribly we misinterpret elementary biology.

As it is an irrational effect, I say again, it would benefit us little to look for its cause in a rational origin. It cannot be a strictly logical set of events that mark the transition from education to stupidity; an illogical fluke is a much likelier trigger. I take it we ought to look for the answer in matters that are not of the mind alone. In this particular scenario, I believe the true culprit to be irrational fear. This is the phobia I referenced earlier in the chapter.

*

When testing for prevailing fallacies, I advise looking at the things people praise despite the fact they do not understand them – not even at a basic level. Ideas they hold in high regard, or ambition they deem too important, something for which they would sacrifice much (their character not least, their principles being first to go), the thing they teach their children to want and the thing they deem you crazy for rejecting. It is important that, despite their obsession with it, they have no idea what it actually means. It also matters that this lack of understanding manifests as confusion in theory and practice alike – if it is a confusion in only one, then it could be a matter of willpower or eloquence instead. But total contradiction is positive for a fallacy.

Of these, a good example proves the concept of alpha males.[8] If you ask some people, they will tell you that an alpha male is responsible, loyal, upholds the law, takes personal responsibility, works for the community, and takes care of his children. If you ask others, they will tell you that it is a beta male who takes care of his children or wastes himself on the community, for an alpha male impregnates and migrates, as he is self-reliant (and therefore appealing) enough to get by without serving anyone – not even his own children, for he has begotten too many to care if any one of them makes it in particular. Everybody wants to be alpha, everybody seems to understand that being alpha is one of the most important things in life, yet nobody has the slightest clue what it means to be alpha. I have seen people try to mystify the expression to mean some entirely unidentifiable quality, unmistakable yet impossible to put in words, the way that drug abusers speak of spiritual enlightenment, or university law professors speak of the law. Others still have tried to make sense of it using something between behaviorism and Darwinian semantics, and have argued

---

[8] (as is the concept of alpha females, however, it tends to be more prominent in the rougher of the two sexes);

that an alpha male, whatever his personal habits or moral standing, is simply a man who attracts women. This is obvious, the interpreter says, from the fact that women are attracted to alpha males! I will not comment on how stupid that is, except to say that the expression remains equally as unclear and equally as desired as ever – everybody wants to be alpha, yet nobody knows what it means to be alpha.

It is fitting, the irony, that there are no such things as alpha males (or alpha females) and beta males (or beta females) among mankind – not even anything resembling such a hierarchy. There are only functional men and women who would not cause harm, and lunatics who would. These latter are in reality cowards: so terrified of taking a risk trusting another, mainly because they know better than to trust themselves, that they will do anything to ensure their own safety. Seeing as they are not very intelligent people, their means of ensuring their own survival (or anything else really) tend to gamble on destruction. It really is that simple. There is no point trying to reconcile poor scholarship in the study of wolves to some Darwinian reality in an entirely different species – a significantly more complex, intelligent, moral species at that.

This should not have been that hard to realize. That young men fall for it is not surprising on account of their underdeveloped brains, but that adults should encourage them in such pursuits is indicative of brains that are, in an etymological sense, very much retarded. If these so-esteemed alpha males really were the born leaders of the pack, it does not make sense that it is these same alpha males that pose the biggest threat to the group they are supposed to have been born to lead. A man looking to start a fight is not a dominant male putting a submissive male in his place, but a coward having calculated that the odds are in his favor. You would think the leader would prefer to employ his brawn to protect the group instead of threatening its members. A man sleeping with many women is not a superior male fit for mating, but an over-compensating child. I assure you, a man confident in his ability to attract women would have the ability to say *no* to some – to most of them even, before he has met the right one. And the stereotype regarding men flouting their wealth, their expensive cars in particular, cannot have come about for no reason at all. These interpretations are hardly controversial, although they now constitute the less preferred take – the dated, beta-male take.[9] For many people, it is a world of alpha males doing alpha male things, and beta-males who must endure it lest they become yet a third or even a fourth genre of suboptimal male.

This new string of mythology has a far less flattering origin than the macho nature of the masculine gender. It has to do with domination. It is a weird subject that I have never fully understood. I never thought it made a lot of sense, even when I believed in alphas and betas. Outside the bedroom, where it may be a preference as unorthodox and as common as any other, there is really no factual pleasure to be derived from dominating another person. It is certainly not physical pleasure, and, psychologically, that one should derive an intangible satisfaction from the act answers very little until we have discovered its drive. In nature, there is no reason to assume that one dog would bully another for the hell of it. There are no good arguments either for some deep-seated knowledge (*an instinct!*) among their kind that one ought to be alpha. It is no use to conceal one error with a deceptively meaningless expression, and the other with proven nonsense. No, the only reason we see one dog bullying another must be explicable in dog-terms. With that in mind, and as far as I understand them as a species, I reckon that one dog *dominates* another probably because the latter would do the same to him if given the chance. Being the rapacious creatures that they are, it seems a likely explanation.

---

[9] There are people who believe they can explain all this as proper alpha male behavior; if you meet them, they will argue like so: an alpha male bullies other men to weed out the weak males of the pack; he sleeps around in order to impregnate as many women as possible with his alpha male genes, and he drives a big car to prove it. But I think I have offered enough evidence that the alpha-male mentality is for idiots. You don't need further proof.

But consider mankind. Would we all bully people if given the chance? Do we have the amoral, greedy nature of dogs – would we strangle our own brother, copulate with his wife, and gorge while his children starve? I am sure that some would, but not most of us. It is all the more revealing then, that it is the alpha-minded bully who is the most likely to commit the aforementioned atrocities. The person most likely to suffer such an assault, ironically, is the person who would never hurt another. Not only is it a misunderstanding of one's fellow man, but compulsive action birthed out of stupidity: domination is but immoral behavior arising out of fear, moreover, fear that is not even a little rational. It is fear for oneself, and fear *of* oneself, projected onto others.

The flattering alternative, in all its forms, was a myth all along. There was never any real proof for it, but the insistence that it cannot (*it must not!*) be disproven. It has been illogical at every level, and yet readily accepted, because a coward, cowering as he does from most things in life, cowers from the truth as well.

This is the alpha male mentality. It is no coincidence that, as people's trust in their own kind decreases, as we forget about love and so we learn about fear, and neuroses become the norm, so is there an increase in those qualities we have fancied the qualities of alpha males: indifference, lack of commitment, aggression of all kinds, self-centeredness, ambition in matters of scarcity, boasting, and the most potent coping mechanisms necessary to mask it: obsession with an overflow of pleasures, such as sex on the natural end, and substance abuse on the other.

*

Regarding this chapter, the anti-intellectual will write it off as a meaningless affair. It is not worth his time, he believes, for so functions his misunderstanding of choice. He has convinced himself that intellectualism has run its course. Now that we know that it is all about copulation, for so we believe, we have no use of thinking any further, and so we act.

Next, let us remember the same toxic treatment as it is employed against beauty: beauty has been written off as a misfire of eroticism, a waste of time, or just so much pretense. It is a thing for feminine men and weak-minded women; a thing to be discouraged and abolished; unprofitable; inferior to just about anything else; so relative that it may be hideous yet well-reviewed; a matter to be either ignored or repurposed as propaganda. Is it not the case that such are the opinions of those who do not understand art – visual, aural, or contemplative – people who would rather not acknowledge the voice that carries it, who will not accept a greatness they cannot achieve, who cannot face the world with passion for passion makes man vulnerable, and the world is a dangerous place? In short, of men who fear beauty?

At last, if toxic behavior against men is an attempt to compensate for one's fear of mankind, and, in matters of art, its denial indicates fear of experiencing beauty, then toxicity against intellect is in all likelihood an attempt to compensate for another kind of insecurity. And in that observation is the conclusion that ties this chapter into a definitive revelatory bundle: people hate intellectuals because they fear intellect. I said earlier ("The Right to Reality," *An Essay*) that stupidity and insanity are one, in that stupidity is a kind of insanity, and here I say that stupidity and cowardice are of the same cause. I also said that insanity and immorality are identical, in as far as an immoral person is by necessity an insane person. And here I call immorality an act of cowardice, which is itself stupidity. It is a system of ignorance, fear, and ever-diminishing ethics in lieu of natural sensibility. At its center is detachment from reality. That we live in a mad world is hardly a metaphor.

Into the Fortress

Having looked to the right, let us quickly look to the left, whence we came, and remind ourselves of some of the questions raised during the course of the previous book, and the inferences made answering them, beginning with the most important notion for civilization as we know it (or assume we know it): the postulates by which man may call himself free – summarized in the creed of liberty, equality, and brotherhood, which are as one, and inseparable from sanity and intelligence, which are also related by necessity. Let us then remember the four tyrants (or the four ministers): the first three being the belief that we ought not to think, the foundational propagandic creed that only certain people are allowed to tell us what we get to think, and the conviction that we can think whatever we want; the fourth tyrant was a kind of conceptualization that merges all three into one, and by which man loses his claim to rationality – first to its exclusivity, then to the ability altogether. At last, let us not forget the importance of concept, for it is where generational knowledge keeps living in opposition to the tyranny of time. It is stupidity that allows the loss of freedom, and it is neglect of language that enables stupidity.

And now, looking right again before we cross the road, we see art, the bard's specialty, as a semantic stronghold; robots seek to undermine it, and hordes, apathetic as they are, walk indifferently by it, ravaging the fields by which the citizenry of art sustains itself. It is within these walls that we must first establish our base.

Bards

On the Orphaning of Pleasure

I do not consider myself an enjoyer of George Romero's opus – at least not of his most popular work. This is, of course, by no error on Mr. Romero's part. While I consider him a talented director, by the time I was born, his horror had become a matter of legacy, not a source of unparalleled entertainment. It was while looking into his work, however, that I found a film that has impressed me with its artistic competence, though in a genre seldom associated with art or intellect, and a title that, upon first viewing, I expected would be a silly action comedy, not a spiritual character study. I am talking about *Knightriders* from 1981, part-drama and part mockumentary about jousting bikers, led by a medieval nerd with a name most fitting for a medieval nerd, this being King Billy, played by Ed Harris.

There is a scene where the king talks with some of his friends (some knights, others friendly outsiders), about the financial difficulties the troupe faces, as he rejects an offer for an easy income. When confronted with how hard things have really got, and so how wise it would be of him, according to his collocutors, to make things easier by taking the money, he answers that it is a common problem he notices in people – the way they abandon things when things get tough – their lifestyles, their jobs, their families, their god, their own selves. He does not believe in selling out, even as things get hard. It is a matter of fortitude, of course, a knightly virtue if there ever was one (being of the seven heavenly virtues), that drives knightly decisions, and King Billy is the first of his knights. He adds that he does not agree with the adage that one must first get by in life and only then tend to his ideals; he believes a man ought to fight for his ideals, and so, though he does not live forever, his ideals will live on. This should be a self-evident truth: if a man values his beliefs, he would not sacrifice them on account of his comfort. Our protagonist will not be called a hypocrite.

I admit, it is an absurd exposition, seeing as King Billy's ideals include medieval reenactments with bikes and some new-age iteration of Arthurian knighthood. It is for these games of pretend that he sacrifices his life. In the minds of many watching the film, he is a manchild. In the eyes of most, he is insane. In the film itself, however, he is neither. King Billy is a very real knight in a setting where knighthood has been forsaken – for the duration of the film, he may as well be the last descendant of Camelot. Though born as a twentieth century American, he has no interest in money or fame or president politics or even country. His sole interest is to live life according to what he believes is the right ideal, at once ideally American and entirely unlike the stereotypical American, the perfect hippie, too morally strict to appeal to other hippies. Being the first of his knights, he works to lead his knights to greatness. King Billy's insistence on historical accuracy (never minding the bikes), with strict rules, with honor, and with tradition (again, despite the technology he gladly accepts), is the result of neither random obsessions nor irrational compulsions – and no, being a nerd has nothing to do with it either. It is rather about the things in which he believes being things in which he *truly* believes. Even his doctor, though a qualified doctor, he considers a magician, and the doctor himself also believes in magic. Personally, I feel uneasy around people who hold such convictions (bioenergy makes my skin crawl, and so not by any supernatural means), but it is necessary for the plot that the main character's beliefs should be that thorough: our modern biker King Arthur trusts modern Merlin with a PhD. Billy is not a charlatan, he is not a manchild, and he is not insane: he is too consistent, too logical, and too functional for such accusations.

Near the end of the film, King Billy hands over the crown to his challenger, now that his challenger has turned his back on money and fame, having previously witnessed the fakeness in their pursuit; proud of his knights for keeping their honor, he bids them farewell; he goes on to enact vengeance on an abusive policeman, and gifts his sword to a fan (a schoolkid), before moving on elsewhere, now that he has accomplished his mission on Earth. For many, that last decision is supposed to cement the message that King Billy is not of sound mind, but please do not forget that this is a movie, and an insane character in a work of fiction is not an insane character in real life – he just might be saner than most, provided the theme allows it. That King Billy decided to end it once he saw his mission accomplished is not evidence of insanity, but congruence with his beliefs: there is not much left for him to do down here, and his ideals can live on, now that he has designated a worthy successor.

But it is the scene where he hands over his sword that I want to discuss next. It is during an ongoing pledge of allegiance that King Billy walks into a classroom, interrupting the process, rudely in effect but innocent in intention. He gifts the kid his sword, and he walks out. While some might find such behavior a bit *too much*, this scene captures the most poignant point of the film: it is all play! Just as King Billy plays a knight and a king, just so we play citizens patriots and law-abiding people and alpha males and leaders and lovers and, well, just as he walked the path of a medieval knight, just so we walk our own paths, with our lifestyles and countries and families and gods and ourselves whatever *ourselves* might mean. We differ from King Billy mostly in taste, i.e. in what we prefer to play, not in the fact of playing. It is in our nature. If we are to make sense of things, we must pretend that things make sense. Consider, how does pledging allegiance to your country in a classroom differ from pledging allegiance to your king at a fair? The one is identical to the other – a mere few hundred years ago, Billy's practice would have been the norm. Your country is not really a person present in the classroom, nor is the allegiance you pledge as a kid something to which you would necessarily agree as an adult – to add to the silliness of the thing, it is not something about which your country cares, seeing as it is not a caring entity (it is not even a sentient entity), though there is such a thing as a government that will hurt you on account of your oath. King Billy is no less a king than the pledge of allegiance is a truly sacred rite.

Now, I am not advising mass dissent – far from it. Nor am I proposing a worldview so relative as to abandon all order or tradition or what-will-you. I merely point to the importance of playing pretend. Because it was in playing pretend, i.e. in pretending that he was an Arthurian knight, that King Billy lived his best life – he was true to his beliefs, he did not cause harm to anybody, and his ideals lived on through all the lives he influenced for the better. That is the second way in which we differ from King Billy, after, of course, our taste in lifelong fantasies: King Billy was truer to his beliefs than the rest of us *sane* people – functionally so, mind you: his mark on the world was entirely good. In a way, the protagonist of this bizarre movie was the *best pretender*: he played pretend, and he won – not by deception, which is cheating, but by making it real. In other words, or as a soft conclusion, King Billy was not a manchild but a proper child: he had chosen a good fantasy, and he saw it through.

*

Now, pleasure is really the first thing we learn as kids. As we grow older, we believe we are taught to temper pleasure in the name of other, nobler goals. It is this latter notion with which I disagree. We are not supposed to temper pleasure. We are supposed to learn about pleasure. We do not go to school to get into the habit of reading instead of playing, but in order to learn about the joy of reading. Without the introduction of new pleasures, the fun in play would get stale. Producing sound by strumming a guitar may stimulate some sense of satisfaction, but it will not last unless you put in the work to learn the instrument properly – it is work that enables the superior variety of enjoyment. When you learn to swim, you learn it for the pleasure of swimming – if you only learn it to potentially save your life, it is for the pleasure of living. I find it a point as midwitty as any when I hear that *it is discipline, not will or love or passion, that gets you anywhere in life – after all, without the discipline to go to work, you will die of starvation,* generally spoken by readers of self-help philosophy, a genre as profound as its target-audience is literate, and at a perpetual deficit to ask if there is any kind of discipline that could make you go to work lacking the will-love-or-passion to live. Whoever made up the myth that we must combat pleasure with duty has not really understood pleasure, nor does he truly understand duty. Pleasure is what we naturally feel whenever we do what nature has predisposed for us as right – keep in mind, not as animals frightened of their true identity, but as men and women enacting our true identity, i.e. our human nature.

When we work, we are not supposed to limit pleasure; we are supposed to enjoy what we do. It is also because of enjoyment that we do it. When your parents taught you to hold a fork and knife or to tie your shoes or to ride a bike or drive, whether knowingly or otherwise, they were teaching you to access pleasure: the pleasure of food, of travel, of sports... learning independence is really learning to find pleasure in life on your own accord. Work is no different. Work is supposed to grant you the pleasures of purpose, of labor, and of belonging. One does not see a conservative romance, that being entertainment that romanticizes the conservative lifestyle, about people who dislike their work – on the contrary, we see them happy at their workplace, well-respected, being friends with their colleagues, enjoying what they do, and returning home to happy families. I am disgusted by the kind of employment that makes employees hate their jobs or toil away as robots – to live each day as if under an extortion law, that they must hand over (at least) eight hours of their own time and replace it with something akin to civil torture. That one must, on occasion, take up such a job is a fact of life, but being a fact does not make it any less wrong. That this appears to be the norm in modern society does not ameliorate its evil. It merely turns a sad fact into a global tragedy: we are denied the thing we are meant to pursue. We are denied the possibility to even experience pleasure in what we call our free time, seeing as a tired person is not a person capable of doing much.

I do not say this from a hedonistic or an epicurean or whatever perspective an acolyte of the base senses might profess. I say it as a man concerned with sense-relations. In particular, as a man who, having realized that we are children at heart, understands how this affects our play: we begin to *pretend* that this transgression is a good thing. We buy into the bully's fantasy. We go on to normalize it and to laugh at people who experience it as the torture it really is – tough as we are, those of us with calloused hooves don't mind the burning coal on which we stand. The problem being, of course, that we forget that we were not born as hooved beasts. The other side-effect of the dehumanizing fantasy is that pleasure becomes a word that means very little. Instead of an experience tantamount to life, i.e. to the very pleasure of living, instead of something so good that people work to experience to its fullest, it becomes, now that work has been turned into torture, but the antonym of labor, and thus restrained to the very basic form of play out of which we were taught to evolve for its own sake.

If King Billy was King Arthur, then I assume that the modern employer, or whatever apologist he has chosen to take his side in the media, advances the setting to the legend of Robin Hood, where he plays King John. Unable to escape it, we buy into his fantasy and try to make it bearable by calling it reality. In it, we make our own mini-fantasies, by which, remaining peasants, we may yet be hard workers and realists and just too tough to complain; on occasion we call ourselves lords or maybe sheriffs, all the while looking upon potential Robin Hoods and Black Knights and rightful heirs to deliver us from servitude, ironically, oblivious to the irony that most alleged saviors are just a different brand of slaver.

It is absurd, as is the fantasy of any bully playing pretend: it is a one-sided oppressive mess. Naturally, there are those who seek to escape it – these being people with spirits not yet broken by bully the king. It is at this point that the fantasy of escape begins to develop into a heroic legend, and a new fantastic movement, a new game of pretend begins to take form: the romantic outcast, the man who was born to lose, the pacifist rebel.

It is a strange premise that we see in *Knightriders*: American bikers, born in a nation born out of rebellion against kings and tradition, having a passion associated with rebellion, obsessing with kings and tradition. I understand the All-American biker. I am not the first to liken a biker to a cowboy – riding off into the sunset, on occasion an outlaw, tough without exception, symbolizing independence and freedom. Bikers are, at their core, a modernized (or evolved) form of that legendary piece of American history. They are American knights, meaning chevaliers, the emphasis being on *American*, the irony being in its antithesis, i.e. in the distinctly American movement at the core of their *knighthood*.

But let us look again upon the speech I referenced at the beginning of this chapter: people getting tired of everything that gets hard whenever it gets hard – the unacknowledged betrayal, alternatively, the self-deception that we value our ideals though we are quick to trade them for comfort. It is highly unlikely that people have always been quitters – that we have always met challenge with hesitance. We would not have survived as a species if we were. I consider it a relatively modern thing, and I believe it coincides with the confusion that we ought to call reality what is in reality slavery, and to call effort or labor or work a thing belonging to this conceptual perversion. I blame it on bad kings – the kind who make peasants perish from exhaustion working the royal fields, perish in battle defending the royal estate, and perish at the stake for questioning royal benevolence. Let us then consider what King Billy does for his band of knights: he fights for them, as a good king would, there are things he provides for them, also as a good king would, and he sets an example for them, again, as a good king ought to. What he does best, however, is that he enables for them a unique kind of pleasure, and a clear set of virtues by which to obtain it. Knighthood in his court is earned through valiance, honor, and hard work. King Billy's court is capitalism if capitalism were not a scam: it is a free market if the market were actually free – free not to do whatever it wants, but free to be what it should be: honorable, virtuous, and fair. Living so against the norm, they are all outcasts – Billy's troupe. But they are not the mindless kind of outcast as are substance-abusers or petty criminals or mere antisocial types that make the experience of reality all the less pleasing. They are outcasts seeking not chaos, but order – they want things to make sense: a king who would not send them to die on his behalf, who would not steal their money, who would not make them toil as slaves. They want a king who accepts them as the knights they are – as noble men, honorable, and worthy of respect. This is the fantasy of knighthood: it is a fantasy of freedom and of duty as one – of individuals treated honorably, and expected to be honorable in return. Contrary to the apparent contrast that Americans should fantasize about knighthood, it is, despite its appearance, the most natural fantasy for a nation built on individuality and freedom.

The person who fantasizes about knighthood seeks a benevolent ruler who will merge labor and pleasure into the unity in which they belong: hard work and excitement and honor and joy; they seek a parent who will teach them to walk, so that they may experience the enjoyment of sport; who will teach them to read, so that they may experience the pleasure of good literature; an authority by which to gain ideals in which name they would not buckle under the threat of pain, because they know there is better pleasure in upholding something noble than either toiling just to live or living just do die.

The opposite is what I call orphaned pleasure. It is the idea that pleasure must be entirely of the self and for the self – even if it is for another, as some men like to boast, it is, ultimately, so that they may feel all the better about themselves; the conviction that if it is a kind of pleasure that is not easy or immediate or necessarily guaranteed, it is a pleasure not worth the investment. It is the development of a feral child. It is pleasure born into chaos and leading to ruin. When base pleasure becomes boring, as it inevitably does, it is to be artificially amplified or boosted in some way, through any inferior iteration disguised as variety. It is a knight without knighthood – a soldier without a cause, a mounted marauder. It is man trying to lead an inhuman life. It is not even a pleasure-and-pain system, as one becomes increasingly jaded, but a system of pain-and-avoidance-of-pain. There is nothing for such a person to enjoy. Our subject's sense of pleasure is like an unfortunate kid, parentless almost immediately after birth, lacking the energy to learn to read, growing weary of his toys, his plushies and his squeakies, the only things he has ever known to associate with pleasure, frustrated that there is nothing bringing him joy.

*

Bards are tasked with bridging the gap between existence as it is and existence as it should be. When we say that it is art and poetry and whatnot that makes life worth living, what we mean is that it is art that makes life into life – it is the difference between what D.H. Lawrence refers to as being "a man alive" as opposed to a "dead man in life." One is to experience life for what it is, and the other is to have a merely casual relationship with it.

We are meant to feel pleasure; art, in all kinds, contains that pleasure in nigh infinite density. That last phrase is not mere flattery: within itself, a piece of art really does contain *all there is* in its instantiation. "For out of the full play of all things emerges the only thing that is anything, the wholeness of a man, the wholeness of a woman, man alive, and live woman" (Lawrence). In order to experience this, however, a man must work. Good art, as all good pleasure, is not accessible by the same means as base pleasures. If you want to dance, you must *learn* to dance, and that is provided you already know how to walk; the good news being that, if you can walk, you will most likely feel the urge to dance at some point – the trick is to act upon it, for it is a good urge.

With that in mind, I will proceed with this section as a treatise on the quality that makes art what it is, namely art as a gateway to pleasure, and what kind of pleasure it really is. I will talk about it as a phenomenon in the modern world – not a form restrained to the bygone era of centuries past, but a thing presently real and developing, along with the standards by which we qualify it and make its ministers worthy of the name.

Meditation on a Replica

Bards cannot do what they ought to if people are not willing to meaningfully engage with them. How could they? It is a sad affair that the work of bards in the modern day is the least successful (or among the least successful) kinds of labor. One might be tempted to point to successful writers to refute this, and write off on poor quality the multitudes of examples to the contrary, but, if he does, one will have failed to recognize the argument from synchronicity: in the present day, among the least successful writers there are writers who, centuries ago, were some of the most successful. Just about nobody really reads Shakespeare; nor does anybody seriously care for Dickens. If not for schools, most classic writers would be getting no sales – save for perhaps the odd purchase because somebody heard good things about them, *once*, then tried reading them, *once*. It is a fact of modernity that we tend to downplay: if the classic writers were modern writers, they would stand no chance of ever becoming classics.

I am not saying that we ought to exclusively read classic literature by the way – far from it; we need to give modern writers the chance, including yours truly. I rather mean to point to the deterioration of the cultural landscape: that writers one cannot simply brush off as *unsuccessful writers* or call them low-quality on account of their poor sales, are nonetheless thoroughly unsuccessful in the present day, irrespective of their talent, of which abundance we have ample proof in history.

I mostly talk about writing because it is the subject with which I am the most familiar. The deterioration of quality in art, however, is observable in all media – in some places more intensely than others, of which writing is, in my experience, the most affected, but the problem is present everywhere, identical in essence though varying in form. Film tends to be either shallow entertainment or pretentiously artsy – not the work of bards, but a doting Peter Greene marveling at his university wit. To be sure, there are some gems, but they are few and far between – either that, or good film does not receive the coverage it deserves. With music, it is not quite as bleak, but this is not to say that, in spite of all the music we enjoy and deem *underground*, there are not countless musicians whose names we do not know and whose melodies are yet to reach us, who far outpace the music we hear on the airways – including the *underground* stuff that is so underground it fills stadiums. There are talented creators who struggle to make a living, and of whose existence we are shamefully oblivious. Between art as entertainment, business, and propaganda, I feel we have lost the sense for telling what art actually is, or what it ought to be.

*

I was meditating one day, practicing what is known as secular meditation. This is not a spiritual experience, but an exercise in control over the loudness of one's mind. You do it by sitting in place for a determined amount of time, focused on but the present moment, and you try your best not to think of anything – if you do get a thought, as you almost certainly will, the trick is not to pay it any mind (let us pretend that pun was intended). This attempted presence of mind in the presence of the moment, to differentiate it from a potential nap in the immediate future, one ideally practices with the eyes open. I prefer to look at objects of aesthetic interest when I do it. And so it happened one day that I was meditating on a replica of a nineteenth century bust, originally credited to a man named Cristoforo Vicari Caslano, that I realized, despite the meditative goal to ignore thoughts during the process, all that I wanted to say about my theory of art. Much of it is Romantic, and I suppose an argument of convergence does apply.

It is a bust of a girl reading. I am enamored with its elegance. I have seen other versions of it, and none have the same grace – in a lot of them, the girl's face is pudgy or stuffy or too wide, and in a

66

select few, much to my dismay, she is painted. I am not aware of the proportions of the original, but if this version differs from it, specifically in the slimness of the girl's face, then I would argue this replica might be superior to the first iteration. And here is the first tell of a good work of art: one can meditate on it. It calms one's nerves, it steadies the mind, and it helps focus one's thoughts on something other than everyday distractions. Note that last bit – it helps one focus, beyond the daily illusion of *problems*, onto the blessing of existence whereby existing is an enjoyment of its own. Art does not dull, nor does it distract. Art stimulates, but only in the purest way. It "brings the whole soul of man into activity, with the subordination of its faculties to each other, according to their relative worth and dignity" (Coleridge, "Chapter 14"). Granted, nature is just as capable of the same effect, seeing as many would prefer to meditate in nature or while looking at pictures of nature, even to the extent that profound thought may be directed at nature (be it in biology or mysticism) in the same way that profound thought can be directed at a work of art, which further proves the point I am about to make next – all art, even art depicting the legacy of man or even alien architecture, though it seems the opposite of nature, is in reality a continuation of nature.[10]

If nature is creation, then art is secondary creation. If what I say here sounds familiar to you, and you are also familiar with Coleridge's take on the imagination, the Romanticism in my convictions becomes evident. Coleridge recognized two kinds of imagination, primary and secondary, with primary imagination being the perception of existence, and secondary imagination being an echo of the first, as we recreate what we have perceived with the ambition to "idealize and to unify" (Chapter 13). We take

---

[10] I do not mean nature in the sense of the environment; by nature, I mean life, in its etymological origin related to Latin *nasci*, meaning "to be born" (Skeat, 344, 638). It is why the same effect is present in many experiences not necessarily related to the environment, but without exception a part of life, meaning that good art is a replica of life – at its purest, and at its most memorable.

reality, and though what we know of reality has been made stale by repetition, we make it fresh through its aesthetic renewal, as we reimagine what we know into a novel form, in which appearance we discover an until then unheard echo of "the eternal act of creation" (Chapter 13). It is in the fact of this regenerative property that art relates to nature.

Nature is a living thing. There is no controversy in that. Now, the thing we tend to neglect about the truism is that living things do not get stale. They are dynamic, they change, they multiply. It is *in the nature* of life that it does not rot. I do not see why this should not also apply on the intellectual level: the knowledge of nature, of life, can never reach a definite halt, whereby we know everything and from every point of view. Not just in science, but in any and every aspect of learning – at the least, subjective experiences are by definition indefinite.

It is only in our uninspired games of pretend that we convince ourselves of the opposite – that learning is pointless, that beauty is horny for illiterate people, that ideals are cope for horny people... it is orphaned pleasure looking to remain in Neverland. Art proves that reality is not quite as bland as it seems to those whose pretense is pragmatism. Art reminds us that whatever boundary we have set up against thought is one of ignorance, not of wisdom; that the things we experience and the things that experience awakens in us hail from a cognitive well inaccessible to shallow proposition, which yields but dry language. To those willing to see this, it enables the sensibility for immense pleasure at every instance of the revelation. The revelation, do note, being of existence, is as infinite as existence itself. It is a talent unto infinity. Hence the praise of the "genius" in the talent to produce "the strongest impressions of novelty" while preserving "the most admitted truths from the impotence caused by the very circumstance of universal admission," or in simpler terms, the skill "to combine the child's sense of wonder and novelty with the appearances which every day... had rendered familiar" (Coleridge, *The Friend* 76).

Coleridge meant this chiefly about poetry, but I think it makes sense to extend it to every kind of art. Shelley went so far as to write that even scientists, in presenting things for the first time, or in coming up with new means to denote reality, spoke in a language that was "vitally metaphorical; that is, it marks the before unapprehended relations of things, and perpetuates their apprehension," and therefore wrote poetry. There is also an instance in which he explicitly references the "plastic and pictorial arts" as abundant in the "instinct and intuition of the poetical faculty." This observation, inclusive though it is, also posits the first stipulation of what art is not, namely the thing Coleridge calls fancy, which stands behind any allegedly creative product that does not meet the above conditions.[11] These "fixities and definities" require little of the imagination, but serve (if I may so paraphrase it) as ornament, potentially pretty, but not poetic or artistic in their own right. Fancy cannot be art, as it does not recreate; it does not renew; it does not seek to understand, to reinterpret, or to find any hint of the eternal. Fancy is not a reminder of the virtues of playing pretend, but just another game of pretend: of whatever we wish to see, whatever desire we want to satisfy, and whatever technique we have learned to the effect. It is present in the kind of art we can tell is not exactly art, in journalistic pathos, in cheap prose and in most song-lyrics: it is present in any creation that, though superficially pleasing, fails to utilize the imagination, first as a means of apprehension, and then as a means of renewal. It is what constitutes the difference between emulation and imitation. In blunter terms, fancy lacks *the soul* present in what we instinctively recognize as art. This is why poorly drawn art can remain art whereas the illustrations in a biology textbook are generally not. It is why some art holds more

---

[11] The basic definition of fancy would be an artificially selected set of notions spliced into a single product for its immediate appeal, in Coleridge's own words, "a mode of memory emancipated from the order of time and space; and blended with, and modified by that empirical phenomenon of the will which we express as choice."

value than other, and the difference between photography as art and a selfie. It is why Jackson Pollock does art, even though I dislike it. Fancy may look nice, and it may capture an image perfectly – a good enough imitation can be lifelike – but art captures the essence of life itself, which is why I call it emulation. I have seen girls reading in person and I have seen girls reading in pictures made to look as beautiful as possible with makeup and lighting and airbrushing, but whereas one is a common sight and the other but ornament on top of the common sight, the sculptor who may have been Caslano (or an imitator thereby) captured in chalk the essence of the act, or its enduring sense of tranquility.

Now that I say it, it sounds trite: tranquility. I have devalued the piece. I do not like that bust for its tranquility. That would be silly. There is a lot more to it, but that is just the thing: mere words cannot fully explain an instantiation of art – a poem might, or a song, but it is best that you see the sculpture for yourself. Without the sculpture, neither elegance nor tranquility will be as clear to us as this specific bust recreates them for our viewing pleasure. There is a philosophical poem by one John Davies that Colredige references in the *Biographia Literaria* by the title "Know Thyself." One of its stanzas describes the soul like so, "Thus does she, when from individual states / She doth abstract the universal kinds; / Which then reclothed in divers names and fates / Steal access through our senses to our minds." If this sounds like art to you, then you are on the same page with Coleridge, who admits that, with slight modification, these lines can apply to the poetic imagination. I wonder if it was under the same influence that Bishop Fulton Sheen got his inspiration, when he said that the mind draws things to itself, and, in so doing, it either increases their value if they are below it (think of a rose becoming more than what it is as soon as the mind makes it into a symbol), or alternatively it diminishes the value of concepts conceptually above it, as we do with such concepts as justice or pleasure or paradise. Now, in regards to the latter observation, art is the means by which we may experience the intangibly lofty without devaluating it – without forcing things too complex for the human mind into distortions molded according to its limits. The poetic quality of the imagination is unique in that it accomplishes this feat while also appealing to the intellect by means of elliptical stimulation, or indirect contemplation. We may yet dwell on the highest ideals in life, not excluding life itself, but without the hubris of intellectual overreach. Like the practice of virtue in understanding what is good, the experience of art allows us to know beauty even though we are yet to agree on its semantics, discussions on which can only cause it to grow less appealing through the dryness inherent to formal iteration.

There is an esoteric implication in this. Any spiritual theory worth its salt (this salt being of the Earth) is open to the idea that what we see of reality is not all of reality: that the observable universe is but one facet of what it really means to exist. They all tend to agree that, when humanity acquires its final form, we will at last know the glory that eludes us from behind the forms: in Christianity, this would be the world restored to its original purpose; to Eastern philosophy, sold as New Age to the western man, that protestant analogy to Buddhism, it would be a vision without the distractions of desire; to a pagan, it would be no less Platonic. With that in mind, it should not surprise us that art works to reimagine the observable universe: we see but a facet of it anyway, and art offers us a glimpse into the many forms to which our eyes have no intrinsic right. But consider next, the moral distinction between pleasures – of good pleasures and bad – and consider art as a pleasure, universally considered good, and its pale imitations, often regarded as bad, and what that implies if we trace a pattern between the two kinds of pleasure and good art, made with the imaginative faculty, and poor imitations of art, which are the products of fancy. For as we reimagine the world in accordance with what it is, an ode to life, we participate in its restoration to what it should be – to beauty beyond the shorthand of the base senses. And by so learning and so participating in such a feat, we include ourselves in this process of restoration, for we also learn about our own selves, as we come to know ourselves in dimensions beyond the limits of the base senses. The pleasure we feel then must be the pleasure of becoming our true nature – the nature we do not know in its fullness, but the nature in which we feel the most ourselves, and for which reason we recognize it as good. Fancy, on the other hand, is but a fanciful perversion of nature – it is what we would rather be without concern for what we actually are; it is akin to eating berries that look appetizing but are in reality poisonous. It is why fancy and its imitations of art are often (not in all cases, of course) associated with bad pleasure: it is not the pleasure of knowledge or of restoration, but a perverse enjoyment of a faulty reconstruction, which is to say a confused, elaborate variant of destruction.

Therefore, art must in all instances be a triumph of the imagination. While it may demonstrate skill, this is only as long as the skill in question exists to uphold the poetic faculty of the piece. It can have a moral, as long as the moral stems naturally from reality imagined anew. It can even entertain, as long as the integration of amusement does not interfere with the artistic duty to remain faithful to reality. Any attempt to smuggle anything else with art only contaminates it; it dilutes the essential substance and, if in high enough amount, it disintegrates it. It turns poetry into rhyme, prose into pulp, sculpture into mannequin, painting into picture, film into footage, life into imitation. Nature does not sell, it does not preach, it does not distract – it merely shows, and it is up to us to perceive.

I will briefly use this paragraph to thank you, Dear Reader, especially if you are of a materialist camp, for indulging my spiritual propensities. I understand the subject causes unease among many. The bias against the transcendental, by which most people reject it, is matched only by the insufferableness of those who profess it. But I would not have written the paragraphs above had I not deemed them essential for our study. Consider, for instance, Socrates' inference in Greater Hippias, when he argues that "neither could the good be beautiful nor the beautiful good, if each of them is different from the other." This is on semantic grounds: the good cannot be but beautiful (ugly virtue is a contradiction), and beauty lacking goodness is not in fact beauty, but an illusion – manifestation without substance. It gives a new meaning to Keats' "Beauty is truth, truth beauty - that is all / Ye know on earth, and all ye need to know." Keats most likely did not mean it in this sense, but do note the unity between the three: beauty, goodness, and truth. They are really one and the same. Even in such expressions as *an ugly truth*, we do not mean to say that it is ugly because it is true – we say it is ugly because it is not good. Likewise, we call *pretty lies* immoral precisely because whatever they state is not factually beautiful. I take it, viewed this way, as good pleasure in imagination and potentially deceptive pleasure in fancy, we tap into an understanding of the world that is due for a revival in casual discourse. It is the fact of unity.

There has been a tendency, as unromantic as any uneducated whim, to separate the three from one another: to make intelligence, on which we rely for the discernment of truth, into a thing wholly separate from the imagination – into a dull, dulling, rather ugly thing producing yet uglier results for ugly purposes; to make beauty a thing virtually antonymous to truth, with whatever ornament a particular society deems beautiful as the substitute to natural beauty. And do note, when it is nature that we are shown, it is as a thing neither beautiful nor good – but an amoral, antihuman, filthy iteration of wilderness. If there is indeed a connection between the rejection of moral values and duties and the ugliness associated with the post-modern world, then it is none other than the rejection of reality for what it is, which is to say the rejection of nature, the neglect of life, and the unity as which we recognize it.

Made of white gypsum plaster, and with the contours of her hair fluffy in the middle and sharp at the edges, I observed, that moment, that the bust almost looked like it was made of whipped cream. One gets weird thoughts when meditating – perhaps it is why we are supposed to ignore them. For a moment I thought, *why not – what's wrong with it being a dessert-sculpture*, and the next instant I knew why: art is permanent. It cannot be a fleeting thing; not by design destructible, i.e. meant to perish. Nature is not a testament to the transience of life, but to the *fact* of life. This random thought of a dessert-bust reveals many truths concerning the qualification for art: it tells us why an advertisement cannot be considered art; why erotica can only pretend to the title and deceive nobody; why a story with a political message is by necessity repulsive; why educational cartoons are not good cartoons, and why sheer entertainment is not art either. None of these forms exist independently; they all have alien, fanciful motives that interfere with the appreciation of life; they do not allow the extension of nature's holistic essence into a legitimate rendition. They stand for the imposition of man onto nature: the distraction of the base urges, of business, of personal ideologies, of deception, of numbing the mind... But art, Dear Reader, pursuing unity, must also pursue eternity (however you understand that word); it must be an ode to life, not a slave to its opposite; there is no place in eternity for making money or killing time or such a fleeting thing as bodily stimulation. Transience cannot maintain the unity that exists in all that exists, namely the unity that is existence itself. Nor can it be called a unity, a thing resulting from the fact of disintegration – whether we run to it as we numb ourselves or we flee from it as we make money by it. The end of things does not unify things in anything – literally, the end of things unifies them in *nothing*. It is poor logic to call inexistence unity; transience only promises to separate things from what they are, and so it is the opposite of unity, as it foretells the end even of the unity of the self – the most primitive cognition of life there is. Art must transcend time.

Looking at the bust, that Victorian relic replicated and sold in the 1980s, I knew: unity must endure; art is not a mere isolated moment of infatuation. It is in art that we see history: the things that influenced the artist as he worked, no less than all that influenced the people by whom the artist came to be; we see his mark on the world, and the world's mark on him. Every work of art testifies for the whole of humanity leading up to it – what the artist knew, what he did not know, what he thought, what he thought important, what he did not think, how he was raised, how the people before him were raised, and how they reacted to it all; in the impression his work has on us, we see those same things in ourselves. Art, epic or concise, profound or funny or masterpiece or just a piece, is the signature of mankind across history. The better the piece, the stronger the signature. I quoted T.S. Eliot in my previous entry, and here I will reference the same text: "Someone said: 'the dead writers are remote from us because we know so much more than they did.' Precisely, and they are that which we know." This is our legacy. And all of it is potentially contained in as little as the slightest glimmer of poetic competence.

Now you know the meaning of what I have elsewhere referred to as semantic compression (*An Essay*; "The Debtor," *Chapbooks Trilogy*). It is also why I called art a substance in which pleasure is contained in nigh infinite density. The two metaphors play off each other. Art is a form of semantic compression because it is an amalgamation of all these things: of the past the present and the everlasting, of groups and individuals as one, of order and of deviation, of characters and personalities and sensibilities; it is stimulation for the mind that answers to a longing of the spirit; it can stir deep emotion and it can be enjoyed independently of any emotion; it simulates the knowable universe with its less than knowable substance, envisioned, communicated, and understood for what it is. Universal in ambition and unique in each manifestation, art emulates creation by being creation, i.e. as close an approximation to its entirety thereby. And all of this in but an image or a set of images or a story or melody or form – in anything, big or small, lofty or modest, complex or simple – high art and art for the everyman alike, all arranged in a celebration of unity, a whole dedicated to the pleasure of its realization.

<u>The Millennial Hill: is all art that ends as Art?</u>

All good artists are patriots. I have written about the role of culture in the creation of art, but this is not about national culture – not entirely. If you have studied history to a degree where you read particular historians, i.e. the interpreter matters to you almost as much as their written interpretations, you might have noticed two trends in historical scholarship that share the same likelihood to cloud a historian's judgment, and so in spite of his or her commitment to objectivity. The first is that, the more pathetic a country is in the present, the farther back in history it must look to justify its value: the more biasedly its countrymen interpret it, the more they obsess with it, the more jealously they guard it. The second trend is that, when a foreign interpreter tries to study the history of a particular country, impartial though he might be regarding the distant past, he becomes precariously less reliable the closer he gets to the present day, especially as he nears a record of his own country's involvement. One trend tends to misinterpret the distant past, and the other tends to misinterpret the near-present. But as far as comparisons go, they are more akin to clones than mere brothers in error, for they are copies of the same fallacy.

The pursuit for a glorious past in times of misfortune is pursuit for a collective reality the affected party would rather have. It is an identity-thing, whereby people do not want to be considered as unimpressive as they presently are. It is no different than the historian from a reputable country becoming less reputable himself as the subject begins to affect his own position – his being right, his support of the good side, his own sense of national self-worth. The ego demands to partake in a flattering reality, its time and place never as important as its glory. It is by no means a matter of patriotism. Chesterton noted of Kipling that Kipling does not love England, though Kipling considered himself a diehard patriot: "He admires England, but he does not love her; for we admire things for reasons, but love them without reasons. He admires England because she is strong, not because she is English" (*Heretics*).

Achievement and ancient glory should not determine a man's feelings for his country any more than should wealth and bloodline determine a person's affection for their partner. As much as I like history, its glorification has nothing to do with love. On that same note, neither is it patriotism to adore your country's natural attractions. Of course, you are free to enjoy your country's natural beauties to their fullest, but you should not mistake this with love for the country itself. Nor is it patriotism to pretend that you have a particular fondness for the people that make up your nation. I assure you, the majority are (by necessity) nothing special. People are just as crooked wherever you go. I repeat, these are not forbidden sentiments. You can be fond of many people in your country, but you can be just as fond of people in any other country – it is not patriotism that stands behind the sentiment. I would say the same goes for culture.

Myself, I am a patriot. I love my country's history, I like our culture and our natural attractions, and I am fond of some of the people here. Nevertheless, this does not make me a patriot for my own nation any more than I am a bigger patriot for foreign nations which cultures natural attractions and people I prefer to my own. My patriotism stems from another notion altogether: it is that, being in the position to learn and to know and to speak my unique understanding of the world – or what I have learned, what I know, and what I preach – I understand that I owe this gift to my personal chronotope: specifically, the fact that I am here *specifically*. I am the product of the people the circumstances and the territory that make up this nation; as you hear me, you hear my countrymen, you hear my ancestors, you hear what they have endured and you hear what I endure – the things that only such people as ourselves may know; when I speak so, I hear them talk through me and talk to me in the same manner. This is not esotericism. It is simple cause-and-effect. It is patriotism in the intellectual sense.[12]

---

[12] There are many senses in which one can be a patriot, of course. Being a law-abiding citizen is patriotism in the practical sense; putting your

If you live in an empire, you can be of unique service to your people as well as to the people of the world by sharing what you have learned living in an empire; if you live in an oppressed country, you know more about oppression than the man from the empire; if you live in a country with too negligible a history, then you know peace better than many. You become a cosmopolitan, of course, when you have acquired the ability to listen to what people of all nations have to say: their histories, their experiences, their ancestry, what they see in life through their own historical cultural and circumstantial character...

This is why all good artists are patriots. It is no use to idealize and to unify what you do not understand (or that you understand only in part), nor is it of any use to idealize and to unify what has been unified and idealized many times over. Sometimes, repetition makes even renewal stale. It is the gateway to cliché. But every one of us is a character so unique that we can all be prophets one unto another, and we would have something new to share with one another even if we were given an infinity of time to do so.[13] People who realize this are the most competent at their work, they make the most valuable contributions, and they are among the most sincere representatives of their nations – even if, believing that they live in oppressive empires, their stances are anti-imperial, and so they outwardly appear to dislike their countries. Whatever their immediate sentiment, they do not deny their experience; they value it, and they represent it as the true account of their character:

------

people before your own interests is patriotism in an altruistic sense; living in your country of origin come what may is patriotism in its true sense. I encourage all forms of reasonable patriotism. Being a discussion on understanding, this essay is concerned primarily with the patriotic manifestation in the intellect.

[13] "Each, as a high priest returning from his Holy of Holies, will bring from his communion some glad tidings, some gospel of truth, which, when spoken, his neighbours shall receive and understand. Each will behold in the other a marvel of revelation" (MacDonald, "The New Name"). This is MacDonald's paradisiac version of the afterlife, which I consider to be the second most appealing way to spend eternity.

a one-of-a-kind phenomenon that they acknowledge has been the fruit of their nation: their designated point in time and space, and the things that have led them to it.

*

But as this section is about art, so has this chapter been about art all along. I wrote the paragraphs above to argue that a one-of-a-kind reimagining of life is contingent on the circumstances that give it birth. It is the same with any kind of art one chooses to practice or to experience: the essence communicated in visual arts is not the same as the essence endemic to the written arts, nor is music *art* exclusively when a poem has been set to melody – rather, it is the interplay of sound and performative talent that accounts for an instantiation of musical art, and its effect is only enhanced by the inclusion of lyrics – not disabled without them. With that, there appears the question of just which modes of creative output, or which means of its expression, are to be considered art, and which are categorically not art. This is the one hill where millennials would make their stand: *comic books and video games cannot be* but *art!* It is also where the generation deservedly derided as boomers tends to err: *comic books and video games will never be art!*

My contribution to the debate is simple: all is art that ends as art. We cannot on good consciousness write something off on account of its medium – most art did not begin as classy, requiring college education to be understood, and revered by critics worldwide, but as lowbrow entertainment, as children's stories, as tribal chanting, as ritual paint, superstition, a pastime for the groundlings... and while not all lowbrow entertainment got to develop beyond lowbrow entertainment, some of it evolved into high art.

Horror, for instance, can be a cheap means to income for cheap producers, but there have been, in the past as well as in the modern day, men of genius who have used the genre to explore the human psyche like none other. In the ghost stories of Henry James, which eeriness is a reflection of whatever troubles their characters, such as oppressive family pride bordering on eugenics in *Sir Owen Wingrave*, or a pretentious society with supernaturally double lives in *The Private Life*, James' horror is not meant to titillate the senses with fear, but to rouse the mind by means of the same emotion. H.P. Lovecraft, presently a cliché, is an excursus on 20th century alienation – it was not a pleasant socialite that saw the masses turning into fish-people or a loner outcast transforming into a demonic wizard; nor was it his bubbly optimism that led him to predict one apocalypse after another, all on the heels of mankind's expansionist triumph; that mankind is an accidental offshoot of the Elder Things' propagation of slave-labor is congruent with what I know of Lovecraft's worldview. Mary Shelley was among the first to do it; though a joke to those who have not read it, Frankenstein is a nightmare for theologians and naturalists alike: is the creator not obliged to secure happiness for his creation? is all creation within nature natural? if man is to play god, would it be right of him to play the Abrahamic god? Film does not lag far behind. There is quality horror if you look for it – and you do not need to look too hard. No sensible critic would regard this rich intellectual legacy and remain convinced that horror is inherently inartistic.

The thing with any kind of art is to approach it as a patriot of the genre: to determine the specific way in which it offers an angle exclusive to the medium. An actor should aim to accomplish with his performance what a writer cannot do with his keyboard; a pianist should convey on the piano what a painter's brush has never captured; and if they can put all these together, then that is all the greater tribute to the unity for which art stands. If a graphic novel can do it, combining visual art with complex narrative, it ought to go for it. If a video game, being an interactive medium, can use this interactivity to capture some essential facet of life in a unique light, then that video game is art. Why should the ambition to entertain make video games categorically not-art, as if literature and film and music are obliged to be dreadfully boring? Why call graphic novels lowbrow whereas short stories and paintings in separation are non-controversial representatives of art? Besides, not all art has to be high art. At the least, even without a contribution unique to the medium itself, some media can be a *platform* for art, such as visual art, animation, acting, writing, music – you name it! Play any esteemed video game and tell me that, though it is not itself a work of art, there was not a talented group of artists working on it. As long as the medium can present a work of art, it serves an artistic purpose regardless if it qualifies as a unique form of art on its own.

Now, the problem with the millennial position is the refusal to accept that, like in cheap horror, the creators of comic books and video games do not primarily care to unify or to idealize or to understand. They look to be cool or entertaining; they look to make a profit; if they try to communicate a deeper meaning, it is usually on-the-nose or shallow (or both); even if clever, comic-book-nerds would not read their comics for their celebration of life, but for the people in rubber suits misinterpreting esotericism, the laws of physics, and believable character development. The overwhelming majority of such products are mere fancy – a lot of them very competent fancy, but not really artistic. Therefore, it is on a case-by-case basis that we determine what kind of alleged art is worthy of the name. Just as there is music that is not art, sculpture that is kitsch, and poetry that is cliché, there may well be a comic book that is art, or a video game that is either the Mona Lisa or the Louvre or something approaching that same standard... possibly.

In conclusion, it is true: all is art that ends as art. The standard, I have described in the previous chapter. I advise having an open mind in its assessment, as long as the emphasis is on the mind – its openness being a temporary modifier, not the sole determiner of thought. If art is an intellectual kind of patriotism, and as intellectual patriotism (any true patriotism) must be reasonable, then art should be the same. Wild as it gets at times, and as eccentric as the artist may seem, at the core of his work is the flow of truth – of none but its rational dimension – from the world into his art and from his art into the mind of the beholder – however he defines it. Because without reason, it is just fancy; but with the mind properly employed, it becomes elliptical omniscience.

The Wagnerian Method

I have talked about the classics, and I am sure that most of us agree on what they are. But I also said I would point to examples of genius in modernity, specifically, examples of art not necessarily accepted for what it is. It is important to make note of the latter, as it is from this group that bards are the likeliest to emerge. After all, Shakespeare was an upstart crow when he first began making a name for himself; his genius is not the result of his immediate acceptance in high class society. Those kinds of people rarely make good art; snobbish as they are, high class society manifests taste by imitation, by singlemindedness, and by exclusivism. By contrast, bards are not of the clergy or the royalty. The legend of the legendary artist has motifs of rebellion and of eccentricity. He is a self-made man. An artist must think for himself. He must reimagine. For this, complicity will not do. Conformism to class, norm, or status will not do either.

As each generation has its own culture, reflecting its own circumstances ambitions and grievances, just so does every generation have a chance at its own genius, different from many others, but identical in the fact of their unity. I will therefore proceed to demonstrate epic artistic achievement in a genre seldom associated with traditional culture or class.

Now, to be fair, there are many who have recognized artistic expression in late twentieth century music, but this chapter is not about rock and roll being art, which I believe only a particular extremity of prudishness would deny, but about rock and roll music becoming high art, if even for an instance, and echoing with everything one might expect of the "esemplastic talent,"[14] perfected in its own unique way, by its own unique means. It is art at its finest and art at its purest. Though many will be unwilling to accept it, and I am sure some of you think I am building up to a punchline (I am not, I am serious), there is pleasure of nigh infinite density in the music I am about to discuss in this chapter.

---

[14] It is Coleridge's coinage meaning "to shape into one" (Chapter 10).

I was barely seventeen when I heard it. I mean it. I was working on a school project I found boring, when my eyes drifted to the TV, the background-noise machine, just as a new tune was coming up on the music channel. I should here add that I was not normally fond of the music channel. My social circle at the time being fans of *classic* rock that is rock in name only, as obscenely trendy as it was, I considered it a more poignant point of rebellion to listen to retro-pop music instead of – to use my sophomore lexicon – grungy headbangers by metrosexual whiners. I understand how that sounds, but I do not think the irony is really there: rebellion is the opposite of all complicity – even of teenage trend. My friends asked to be raped, they *goo-gooed* and *ga-gaed*, and they were avenged like Cain; I preferred to dance in the dark. But as I was saying, the music channel was just ambient noise; it alternated music to which I was indifferent with music I disliked. This was just as well, since the project bored me, and I am not one to waste good music on a bad time. And yet, as I looked at the TV just then, and I read the name of the artist and the title of the song, I discovered a musical gem marking the entrance to a diamond mine; there on the CRT screen flickered colors and out of its archaic speakers howled sounds of inexplicable charm, bizarre though it all was – the lead, the names, the presentation. For one, Meat Loaf is a peculiar choice in monicker. It was not cool or edgy or esoteric. It describes nothing but the anatomy of the singer. I thought to myself *that's a good stage name*. The title of the song was just as unusual, and consequently appealing to me: *Bat out of Hell*.

It is a genre known as Wagnerian rock. It has only one writer representing it, and a small set of performers known for it. They are all immensely talented, and, if I briefly allow providence in my worldview, I would say it is true, what some people say: that this writer was born to write music for these particular performers, and that these particular performers were born to perform this writer's music. You would not be mistaken if you think you have traced a hint of partiality on my end as I write about them. I do not mind.

Nor do I mind the reader being disinterested in this music – I do not think a person ought to like all kinds of art. What a person likes or dislikes is contingent on their taste; the trick is to explain the reason for its appeal or (alternatively) its perceived repulsiveness. This adds sense to preference. If I have a valid take, then whatever partiality might have begun the chapter, it cannot be called the grounds for bias.

But as romantic as my experience may sound, and as much as I have enjoyed Wagnerian rock since, it was really not an instant attachment to either artists or product. I do not think I finished the song – not even the intro – upon that first encounter. I either returned to my project, making a mental note about the musician but paying no mind to the tune at the moment, or I might have gotten up and gone elsewhere – I really do not remember. What I do remember is my gradual attunement to it; at first a curiosity (thinking, *didn't I want to check out this music that one time?* and acting upon it), then an enjoyment of his greatest hits, making it my go-to playlist, and eventually looking for outtakes and demos by the people associated with the genre.

It was when I began to cite the lyrics as uncommonly potent, this being just before I made it my main playlist, that I realized I must explain why this is so: after all, it benefits me little to deprive myself of the pleasure of understanding.

*

These songs are, lyrically, theatrical performances put to verse; musically, they are movie-scores. In Steinman's own words, "I write with a theatrical or cinematic context in mind... in my mind, it's always on a stage or in a film" ("The Artist's Mind").[15] It shows. Film and theater have not only influenced him as an artist, but also constitute part of his opus – conceptually, they are *all* of

---

[15] All direct citations of Steinman's recorded convictions regarding music and art are from this source.

his opus. Sometimes as ballads, sometimes soliloquies, and in a few outstanding examples, dialogues, Steinman's songs are about character, intense and epic. They "start at 'extreme' and go from there." The stories they tell are romanticized accounts of a mythical adolescence; rebellious, on occasion bordering on delinquency (a non-violent delinquency, I should add), and sang about with a knightly nobility in spite of never escaping the American middle class. These are songs about love, bikes, seduction, frustration, and small-town camaraderie. They are songs about life in the late 20th century, though inspired, in no small part, by 19th century literature, folklore, and medieval legend. There is other music like that, I agree, but there is an element to the Wagnerian method that stands out.

"I disagree that its [that of music] only role is pleasure, that's just a by-product. Its main role for me, like all the arts, is to provide heightening and amplification. It should intensify everything." Jim Steinman was a cultured man with a poetic vision, even though some would say he does not look the part. You can trace it in his writing – his understanding of the culture that precedes him, as well as the culture in which he partakes. It is silly and witty and yet insightful, unorthodox but archetypal, as close to being *out of place* while remaining ideally just as it should be. It satisfies Coleridge's condition for good poetry, that it should achieve a "balance of reconciliation of opposite or discordant qualities... of sameness, with difference... the individual, with the representative... a more than usual state of emotion, with more than usual order... (Chapter 14)." It elevates small-town experience to epic proportions, and humanizes lofty concepts like love and the soul and paradise with everyday vocabulary.

Just about every piece has a memorable quirk, unique to the song, and compatible with its theme. *Bat out of Hell* has a memorable intro and a guitar made to sound like a bike, *For Crying out Loud* has a beautiful coda, a pun as its theme, and a dirty joke in the bridge, *I Would do Anything for Love* has *that*, and *Objects in the Rearview Mirror may Appear closer than they Are* is memorable for the title itself in addition to its lyrical leitmotif. *Paradise by the Dashboard Light* has not only a twist-ending, but a slight variation in genre midway through the song. It narrates the sexual advances of a young man through analogous baseball-commentary on the radio; it is an intermission happening naturally in the song, and read by Phil Rizutto himself. As the two teenagers are fooling around in the car, Rizutto begins commentating on a player's advance through the bases (first second and third), "a line shot up the middle," sliding in "head-first" and a "squeeze play." The girl stops her partner just before the player on the radio scores the homerun. It is a passionate setting, as the duet glows "like the metal on the edge of a knife." Unorthodox a simile as it is, its symbolic depth goes only as deep as the listener's mind cares to penetrate. The song approaches its climax with the girl demanding over and over that, if they are to go any further, her partner must promise her his eternal devotion, as the latter tries to dodge the question, channeling either a comedic Broadway routine or an operatic performance lacking all pretentiousness. Singing in unison, the two voices begin to mimic two guitars vibing off each other with a "Will you love me forever" lead and a "Let me sleep on it" rhythm. In the end, the male lead swears that he will love her "till the end of time," only for the two of them to conclude that now, after the event, they are "praying for the end of the time," as the song fades out with "It was long ago and it was far away / And it was so much better than it is today." It is romantically touching, it is unexpectedly funny, and it is all about life: about love, rebellion, and regret. Just like *Bat out of Hell*, its unlikely double, *Paradise by the Dashboard Light* is a hymn to rock and roll music and everything for which it stands. As the story plays out, its melody is everything one may associate with the genre and its predecessors. It is, as I explained two chapters above, understanding, unification, and idealization. This is just one song out of many. They are all of equal excellence – in writing, direction, and execution.

The lyrics in Steinman's songs are often ignored on account of their presentation, but Steinman was a competent lyricist; he may not have been interested in writing about politics or social issues, but he had the wit to explain what he does with eloquence like none other – such that, in his case, I would not mind using the expression *intelligent but not intellectual*. I concur, his thematic scope is rather limited: you will not hear a melancholy song about the Vietnam War or a protest song about the mines closing in Bethlehem. But what you do hear, you can rest assured, will contain clever wording. In *Two out of Three ain't Bad*, the speaker tells his lover that

> You'll never find your gold on a sandy beach,
> You'll never drill for oil in a city street,
> I know you're looking for a ruby in a mountain of rocks,
> But there ain't no Coupe de Ville
> Hiding at the bottom of a crackerjack box.

In cruder terms, he could have told her that, like a grain of sand, he is no different from any other man; like the sewers below a city street, he is *full of it*; that he acknowledges her devotion to seeing the good in him, but there is really nothing of substance to find. Then again, the romantic poetic talent is in the poetization of such common traits by which they lose their everyday crassness, whereas the rock-and-roll poetic talent is the competence to do this with imagery evoking sewers and crackerjacks. One can expect some level of wordplay in just about every Steinman piece. He employs phrases that are commonly used with little meaning, and sees in them a sense that subverts their normative use. "You were only killing time and it will kill you right back" ("Out of the Frying Pan"), or "Everybody's going nowhere slowly / They're only fighting for the chance to be last / There's nothing wrong in going nowhere baby / But we should be going nowhere fast" ("Nowhere Fast").

Now, if rock music is associated with rebellion, then what rebellion could be more thorough than the rebellion against robotic language – against soulless words spoken without sensible intent – against listless air parading as breath? What better tyrant to topple? What virtue is there in rebellion unless it is to challenge that which is, and to so root out that which should not be? Is there anything in direr need of change than the normative defeatism we see all around? "My songs are anthems, calls to action, cries against passivity, initiations by fire, doorways flung open, altars uncovered... In a world full of cripples, the only pure revolutionary act is to get up and dance" (Steinman)!

True values are enduring, and it seems that rock and roll dreams have tapped into such a set of values. Even to the extent that they redeem "from decay the visitations of the divinity of man" (Shelley), as they "strip the veil of familiarity from the world." Teenage memories get boring fast; romance is not quite what it seems as one gets older; the epic is curtailed by the mundane, and rebellion loses its luster in defeatism. But not with music like this: with music that appeals to forgotten pleasures, that retells the true account of memory through sentiment, and that reimagines the idiomatic as universal – that glorifies life, that understands a good deal of it, and that works "to idealize and to unify" (Coleridge, "Chapter 13"). This music is an ideal reminder that our collective game of pretend is growing stale, and that life must not be – it *cannot* be such. It is art in its totality: from conception to completion.

It may have for its subject matter subjects that prudish adults might dismiss as juvenile, but that is just a facet of transposing "the feelings of childhood into the powers of manhood" (Coleridge, "Chapter 4"). One needs not approve of the characters in a story in order to understand their righteous angst. That these protagonists are *suboptimal* in the societal sense does in no way turn the music decadent, for these are the "temporary dress in which his [the poet's] creations must be arrayed, and which cover without concealing the internal proportions of their beauty" (Shelley). Besides, according to the man himself, "They [children and adolescents] are closer to the things in life that are really important... to the jugular, the feverish, the primal, the urgent, the intuitive aspects of being human," and as long as one maintains such sensibilities, "you can still be a teenager at any age."

It is a mythicized account of adolescence, as I said, which is youth imagined anew – reimagined as the challenger to norm that, more stale than aged, seeks to entrap man into an inhuman fantasy. Western culture, as of the late 20th century, has produced its own passions ambitions and grievances, and the generation of bards that sought to respond to it, have echoed, in this genre, with the epic call of the everyman.

Jim Steinman's music is at once a classical (Wagnerian) epic, a Broadway musical, and pure rock-and-roll, this latter being both a 1950's throwback and contemporary 1980's hard rock. I argued that art is about unity, and this is music being in unity with itself. It is a tribute upon tribute while remaining perfectly original. It is a densely contained piece of implicit historical knowledge, all of it welded into a salute to the genre. There is passion in this music that turns each song into a play, each vocal performance into stage acting – if you were fortunate enough to see them on set, it really was a rock-opera they performed. It pays no less attention to the lyrics on account of its musical brilliance. It is poetry along a strategically distorted classical tune. Neither of these is out of place; the choice of words fits the settings, and each story is told twice over in melody and language. Steinman's music is the ultimate evolution of rock and roll. It is how the genre peaked.

I like a lot of the music that came after, but I hold Wagnerian rock to have marked the plateau for the genre. Whatever rock music comes next can only ever be of equal quality in the best (and rarest) of cases. I keep an open mind, of course, but I regard it as the definitive standard. This episode of artistic labor, sometime in the 1980's and early 90's was the point when electric guitars, drums, and teenage angst joined the ranks of Beethoven. I am not talking about metal covers of Beethoven, mind you; nice though they sound to many, it is not imitation I praise – Wagnerian rock is not a copy a cover or an alternate edition, but a contribution.

James Richard Steinman, along with those who performed what he wrote, did not approach classical music as pretenders to its greatness, but as worthy inheritors. In so doing, the Wagnerian composer pulled the entirety of his popular-level influences, rock-and-roll blues pop doo-wop funk and even country music, into the same potential greatness. I will say it again: all is art that ends as art.

Do note, however, that, whereas it is good that all things may someday end as art, art ending is an entirely different and an entirely bleak affair. For it has not been Steinman's legacy that the majority remembers when they praise classic rock. It is rather a commercialized subset of a simplistic, hedonistic, stubbornly crude kind of thrashing and banging and angry yodeling. It has been orphaned pleasure that has largely dictated the development of rock music. It has been a philosophy of *what sells* that determined production and a philosophy of *what gets me excited* that has determined fame. Its ideal evolution cut short, the genre has built a legacy that is exactly as its prudish critics wanted it to be: an offshoot of generational decadence.

The marginalization of good art is also why a lot of things that could have been art end before they get the chance to end as art – it is business on one end and orphaned pleasure on the other. Bards face challenges that only their audiences can help them overcome. But numerous as they (the challenges) seem, and as obvious as most of them must be to the reader, it is only one danger that threatens to uproot art altogether – not one genre after another, but the concept in its entirety. It is bound to do the same to the rest of humanity if we let it have its way with art.

Blind Adversity

It is apathy: a problem that the afflicted most commonly misunderstand. They say that they are not in fact apathetic – they can certainly feel emotion and even passion: they love their children, they are happy when something good happens to them, and some may even call themselves sentimental; they have been moved by emotion, they believe, even by the banal, such as when watching sports or a sad movie. Others unashamedly call themselves apathetic, and they see nothing wrong with it. The latter are at least honest with themselves, but, between the two, neither group understands what that word means – else they would not be apathetic, for apathy is an evil only an idiot would consider acceptable within anyone, let alone oneself.

I was originally going to write about the many oppositions imposed upon artists by contemporary modernity. I was going to go onto an epic excursus regarding the problem, beginning with Chesterton's prediction when he said that "the improvement of advertisements is the degradation of artists" ("Utopia of Usurers") because "the artist will work, not only to please the rich, but only to increase their riches," like just another workhorse. I have experienced it myself. Between the mechanical work officially referred to as art I used to do for my employer, and a cheap commission I drew at a later date, it is the memory of the latter, of the *patron's* reaction to it, that I cherish, and the former, in spite of the pay, that I keep in mind only as a *lesson learned*, so to speak. It is the "small-minded cynicism of our plutocracy, its secrecy, its gambling spirit, its contempt of conscience," as the uncheated prophet foresaw, that is the root cause for art turning soulless, as "the artist-advertiser will often be assisting enterprises over which he will have no moral control, and of which he could feel no moral approval..." to which he will have to "bend the proudest and purest of the virtues of the intellect, the power to attract his brethren, and the noble duty of praise."
I thought of a possible objection to this, an imaginary reader thinking to himself: *So what? What's wrong with that: we have economized art – it's a good thing really, because now artists can make money!* as if he had not read a word of what I wrote above. For one, artists cannot make enough money now that we are a dime a dozen, seeing as it is the dime our patrons prefer to art. But the real problem with art as advertisement, I have described in another chapter: art cannot be but for art itself – any other purpose pollutes it. Would you call it a celebration of life if its purpose is as fleeting a thing as mammon; could you call it a reimagining of the world if art itself has been reimagined according to the world; can it be a

sincere creation when it has been begotten with the intent to seduce? It is no coincidence that love and friendship and family and patriotism and liberty all mean less the more you see them in advertisement – financial and political alike.

I was going to connect this plight of our spiritual sensibilities with the spiritlessness of the age, with dead-end jobs and demoralizing circumstances – I was going to use John Ruskin as my point of reference: "you may make use of the other faculties, and let the artistical one lie dormant... there may be two or three Leonardo da Vincis employed at this moment in your harbours and railroads," however, "you are not employing their Leonardesque or golden faculty there, you are only oppressing and destroying it." It is not just the artist to whom this applies, but to any practitioner of distinctly human capabilities. You may have the Brontë sisters working two shifts each to balance their student loans with rent, Bertrand Russel waning in accounting, or George Washington behind a cubicle in Long Island. Sure, we can still practice in our free time – indeed, most art begins as a hobby – but this will not be to the full capacity to which we can develop what we do best. Perhaps it sounds banal on the surface, but do consider the implication, the unspoken fact of its tyranny: that art – and all that art entails – is second to our responsibilities to *the man*: to making him richer, to furthering his power, to convincing ourselves and others of his benevolence on account of his finances. The recreation of the world must wait while there is yet money to be made. It is not mankind that takes priority. Our best talents take a back seat to making rich men without vision – spiritual convicts, if you will, living in "a prison / whose only horizon / is profit and loss" (Bogle). All means of getting in touch with the restorative faculty of the mind are being subjugated to the profitable order – just look at what has been happening with scholars, and you will see the same pattern emerge. Even scientists have morphed from inventors to cash cows.

I was going to make an epic chapter out of that – perhaps even a full section, and used many examples, upped the vitriol, and rounded it off with a conclusion which emotional weight I am presently lacking the eloquence to demonstrate; but I do not think I need to. For one, to those who care, these issues are self-evident. People willing to think on the subject will come to the correct observations on their own. It is not hard to figure out what burdens the modern artist: about the same things that bother the modern non-artist. The indifferent, however, will not benefit (intellectually or otherwise) from anything I have to say here, regardless of how detailed I make it. It is not their concern, and so it might as well not exist. If you would indulge me, it is "A standoff of love, a duel most hellish, / Recognition at gunpoint, fire if you please" (*Chapbooks* 105). Apathy is the toughest challenge for the world as a whole, and it is the bard that feels it the most intensely, even when its manifestation is outwardly mild.

*

Nobody wants to be ignored. People who share their hearts and minds the least. Apathy is the most potent means of ignoring somebody. It is a mode of thinking (and being altogether) by which things that do not affect the apathetic party are condemned to irrelevance. It is oblivion if oblivion were lunacy, lunacy being a rejection of reality. It is an orphaned pleasure begetting bastard children, hardly childlike, and irredeemably immature. What kind of person could ignore the suffering of others, take it so lightly as to even take pleasure in it, and, blind to the irony, call himself the *fortunate* party – the sane, well-situated, well-off intelligent prosperous party? As if his deficiency does not make him ten times as pathetic as those who endure the suffering he is too stupid to perceive, even in himself, living as he does, detached from the one reality he ought to know? That cannot be a real person. Personhood entails recognition of personhood, which itself entails empathy. There can be no such thing as selective empathy any more than there can be selective personhood. There is no use, like that first group of apathetic people, to think oneself normal for caring *some* of the time. That is a simulation of personhood, not actual personhood – it is what an android might do.

I am not telling anybody to either get sentimental over everything or else go beep-booping into the looney bin, but it is precisely that kind of misreading of the chapter that proves what I said above: people misunderstand apathy. They misunderstand apathy because they also misunderstand empathy. For it would be even worse news for one's character if one were capable of feeling empathy as an emotion, but chose not to act upon it regardless of the emotional compulsion. That would be a person who does not trust his senses to tell him wrong from right. It would be man in his least natural state, whereby, not lacking any biological virtue, has chosen to nonetheless rebel against nature; like a man with good eyes, and in good lighting, walking deliberately into a wall. On the other hand, being able to feel empathy as emotion and uncritically acting upon it is not a moral quality as much as a safety hazard. No, empathy should not be the whim that controls us; nor should it be a whim we ought to inhibit.

Empathy is a sense, and as all senses have stimulants, it is by its reception of the stimulant that the organ is proven functional, deficient, or dead. It is this that apathetic people fail to realize. It does not matter what you feel at what you see; it only matters that you interpret it for what it is, and that you act accordingly. Empathy is your most intimate sense for life – all life. That is why it is so well-attuned to art – the celebration of life. The failure to recognize life in any way is a symptom of its degeneration. Apathy is a sickness. Only the insane don't mind being mentally ill.

*

They make for a tough crowd. One cannot, with pleasure, write draw or sing knowing that one will not be read seen or heard. I understand there have been artists who did, but I am talking about bards, not just any artist – bards being artists of the people and for the people. Indifference takes the sap right out of us. It is not exactly discouragement in the form of success denied; it is rather discouragement in the sense of pearls and swine, except that, it feels as though the swine had already launched off the cliff by the time we've had the chance to cast our pearls – we do not even have the privilege of fighting those who will rend us, for they are well-fed and soaring the skies. To the descendants of humanism, indifference feels like a world without posterity.

It is also an apathetic apologist who would raise objections with this chapter. It is in their interest to shun pleasure lest they perceive a reality they will not accept. I can predict them denying my thesis altogether with a pretense to rationality: *we feel pleasure as an evolutionary aid to the propagation of the species, not because we exist to experience pleasure! There is no teleology beyond horny and happy!* Why they have, if such is really the case, on the one hand, so successfully cracked the system as to sense no meaningful life in their fellow man, but they have, on the other, so little power over it, that they remain slaves to just about every other sensation to the same effect, they are yet to explain. But really, this objection is not worth addressing for the fact that it does not present any reason to justify its proposal. It is an unprovable thesis. Just another instance of gross extrapolation, turning the valid theory of biological Darwinism into a social pseudoscience. All the while, it seeks to undermine a set of senses with which we cannot part. It needs better evidence than arrogant assertion if it is to have any merit – intellectual merit, that is, as merit in practice it cannot have, seeing as it only stands to destroy it.

Then again, it is hopeless to discuss with an apathetic audience, because the one thing they can do to make the changing of their minds at all possible, is also the one thing they positively will not do. It is altering the choice that stands between whim and belief into a practical choice: the decision to be good – in particular, to abide by the moral goodness I described in the previous section; the one that is not an arbitrary set of rules, but a system developed, with visible continuity, alongside our conviction that we are rational entities with reasonable faculties we can trust, and so through historical trial and error. If they were to try it, they would, through experience, learn that even an indifferent savage may yet warm up to civilization. But they will not, and so, misunderstanding persists – first in choice, and then in every whim the apathetic choice allows.

The rest of us know this already. Therefore, let us not dwell on it. We will address our robotic counterparts and their so-esteemed intelligence in the next section. For now, let us remember our appreciation for the bards before us, and make note to help out the bards among us.

*

We only need remind ourselves of one thing: that in all instances of living, we play pretend. We know too little of the world not to rely on this leap of faith: we understand it, we are adults, we know what we're doing... There is nothing wrong with that, of course, as long as we see it for what it is; because a good game of pretend always has some bit of truth to it – a bad game of pretend, by contrast, leads to injury, to fights breaking out, to learning all the wrong morals. Ours is no less a reality where everything "selves – goes itself; *myself* it speaks and spells / Crying What I do is me" (Hopkins), than a senseless reality of molecules, cells, and delusions of sentience. Both are fantasy, differing only in quality and phrasing, or the tastes of those who think them.

Not neglecting to learn from the masters of playing pretend, we must observe that children have developed a keen sense of knowing which part of their play they ought to take seriously and which part they ought to view without so much passion. I am telling you this partly in reference to the Wagnerian method. There is a hardcore rock-and-roll crowd that is really not worthy of the music. People with ponytails and leather jackets riding bikes and getting tattoos, on occasion playing guitars and not giving a damn about the norm being what it is and their duty to oppose it.

They unashamedly admit that they only *pretend* to believe in the concept (the essence), though the ornament they take seriously. They are adults, they believe, and so they do not fall for the idea behind the music they so admire... but the looks and the style and the toys associated with it – now *that* is something for which they bleed, sometimes literally. Bards are useless to people like that. People like that would have more use of a babysitter.

Now, children playing tend to take their fantasies very seriously – they can adopt different names, they can get passionate about imagined problems, they can feel fear and joy at fantastic outcomes, and they bond as they play... but do note that they do not take their toys seriously, in the sense that a kid will not confuse his toy sword for a real sword and try to use it for self-defense, or consider his action figure a real person. In instances like these, the young understand ornament better than adults do. Practicing, as frequently as they do, their skills to play pretend, and encountering ornament and fantasy and concept as they learn about life, kids have had the chance to observe just which "Castles fall in the sand,"[16] and can so tell apart what remains from whatever fades in the air.

---

[16] "It ain't right, it ain't fair / Castles fall in the sand / And we fade in the air" (Steinman, "Good girls go to Heaven").

Robots

The Superficial Threat

In this debate, there will always loom the same grounds for disagreement that have arbitrated the discussion even as it first began to take form, threatening at every step to derail any ambition of persuasion, first as a theme in science fiction, for the most part uninformed, and, no longer constrained to fantasy, remains just as ill-informed, despite the time it has had to catch up, and in spite of the gravity of the conclusions being made. I am talking about the apologetic argument from profit. It goes without saying that artificial intelligence technology promises to (and in all likelihood will) boost the profit of many businesses, mainly by cutting down on staff needing salaries, and, as such, it is technology with a perpetual appeal to the capitalist: as conservative a Christian as the red-blooded demographic spawns, he is all for God family and country, occasionally confused at the three bizarre ways to spell mammon, but thoroughly loyal to God family and country all the same.

Such men will try many arguments to convince you why it is a good thing, their overreach against labor: from the dismissive cop-out that AI will create many new employment opportunities,[17] to the citing of statistics, presumably sound, about how robots promise an increase in profit for the business-owner to spend on (no doubt) the noblest of endeavors. You can tell that it is a divisive argument when a good chunk of my right-wing audience has been compelled to close the book upon first sensing my criticism, seeing as to argue against the pursuit of profit is to argue against the one creed they will not negotiate. To them, the question is not about artificial intelligence or human suffering (it never

---

[17] In case anybody hasn't figured it out, a few positions in maintenance and prompt-writing are hardly many new employment opportunities compared to the mass firing of just about everybody else.

was), but about continuing their favorite game of pretend: the Cold War is still waging on, and there is a system they must uphold at all costs, for it is of the good guys, and in which name too much blood faith and crime has been invested to turn back now. Therefore, if an argument against profit is to make sense to them, it must be an argument that is, at the same time, an effective argument against the status quo which they mistake for a moral constant. To even begin explaining why the robot is as demonic an excuse for invention as demonists have ever mistaken for progress, I must open with a brief overlook of the most insidious of capitalist lies – a truism to many, and, as most political truisms, in reality a mischievous fabrication: capitalism has made work noble.

For the record, I am not a communist. Believe it or not, financial liberty is not synonymous with the desolation of human dignity. In right-wing circles, however, any criticism of this kind is associated with an unwillingness to work, freeloading or just general laziness. There is no other reason to dislike it, they insist, for under capitalism, anyone has the ability to work for a better life, as even a poor man can, in theory, make millions, and a rich man can, with increasing likelihood, gain immortality. It is the only system under which, they conclude, one can live freely. Those who hold these beliefs fail to ask themselves why, if socialist thought is tantamount to a dislike of work, socialist movements have always been associated with the working class. The lack of self-awareness in this begins to nudge reality into satire as one realizes that most capitalists do not really get a whole lot of work done – the idle rich, trust-fund babies, the inheritors of businesses... none of these are people who have labored hard or have taken significant risks for their wealth. Though some might argue that kids who inherit businesses are made to work by their parents (often starting at the lowest positions), the idea that they actually work hard is among the cheapest of shams: seeing as they work with the prospect of inheriting the company, whatever job they start out doing, and however strenuous it might seem at first, in the long run, their payment is indefinitely higher than the salary of the worker who, functioning as a mere worker and entitled to no inheritance of the business, stands to gain but his regular paycheck. When one considers the ratio between labor and gain, the boss's kid does virtually no work at all, even if for a short while he is bathed in sweat and makes sure everybody knows it. This is in addition to better schooling and living conditions that further cement the fact of unfairness, though capitalist pundits like to preach about *equality of start*. Under capitalism, work has no liberty-defining property but for those already born free, i.e. free to exploit the rest of us.

But let us take this argument to the discussion at hand: work and robots. You will see how it all comes together. As is the vision for this book, let us consider the problem conceptually: just what does it mean to work? As I write this, I engage in cultural and intellectual labor. Then again, unless I can sell thousands of copies a month, I cannot even cover my bills working as I do, let alone hope for a better life. For this reason, the capitalist considers what I do a self-indulgence, not work, never minding the labor through which I go, sacrificing (or dare I say risking) what would otherwise be my free time. Even the great Mario Puzo admits to feeling guilt at having written a masterpiece that did not sell. "I concluded that I had worked ten years of my life in sheer self-indulgence. I thought myself that most despised figure in Italian culture, a "chooch" – that is, a man who could not earn a living for himself or his family." If not for romanticizing crime later on, he would have likely remained that despicable figure in Italian culture. Just a short while ago, I spent time in education, which, in spite of being the pinnacle of intellectual labor, investing hours in classes and private study and research, has been so removed from the concept of profit, that I would have been financially better off doing entry-level jobs, keeping my brain idle at the expense of the rest of my body. Now, I am not the kind of elitist to degrade manual workers as inferior, but, do note that it goes both ways – to call the student lazy and the cashier hardworking is to call the brain useless and fast-food culture. In spite of the student's intellectual labor, however, the capitalist looks upon him as but a self-indulgent, entitled slob – doing no kind of work whatsoever, and wasting money instead of making them. Clearly, to the capitalist, it is not work alone, but a very specific kind of work that is to be considered *true* work. It is what they deem *productive* work.

Now, on its own, that distinction does not really solve anything, seeing as to call intellectual labor unproductive on the grounds that it does not sell is to call drug-dealers productive citizens and make students leeches. The fact of satisfying demand should not be an intellectual metric of anything. But let us indulge the party of *cold, hard reality* and allow them their stipulation that a product (or service) in demand is the only qualifier for productive labor, and so pose the question: what if I were to live off my land? Such goods have been in demand since the Neolithic. What if I were to plant seeds and breed animals and be as self-sufficient as most men my age dream of being? Indeed, what if? Surely, the capitalist pundit agrees that working the land is productive work. Then again, was it not the ancestors of the modern capitalist that had my ancestors move out of the countryside and into the city? Was it not his team that caused a mass exodus of people into urban dystopias, far from clean water and fertile soil, turning wheat fields into city streets? Were artisans not all but extinguished by modern capitalism? Was it not the capitalist himself, the icon of progress that he is, that made this self-sufficient alternative an impossibility? It is largely thanks to his former actions that what both sides agree to call work is now unworkable. Then again, while he has a lot for which to answer (though I would not hold it against him were he any less self-righteous), my argument is not meant to build up to an accusation. Rather, it serves to bring to attention the perversion of the concept of work: that if intellectual work is by and large not regarded as work, and work of tangible produce is impossible for the average man since he lacks the means to meaningfully engage in it, then the only kind of *valid* work in the modern day, this being labor that could allow a man to earn a living, is, for the majority of the population, an occupation that depends on an intermediary between the labor a man puts in and the payment he gets out of it.

In other words: in order to make a living, one is dependent on one's employers. The modern definition of work is not tantamount to labor, but to employment.

We all long for a society where work is the means by which one lives – his guarantee for survival, for freedom, for security (financial and otherwise) resting solely on the *sweat of his brow*. This is something for which labor parties have argued and bled. There is no point of contention between capitalism and its critics regarding the claim that a man ought to work. The contention is that capitalism has imposed its own fantasies onto the concept of work, and selected a one-sided interpretation of labor as the sole means to a living wage. Consequently, we are deprived of our independence. We do not work to live. We get employed to live. We do not produce anything (or serve anybody) to make more money. We produce (and serve) to make our employers more money. In turn, they let us live. Any attempt to get out of the system is a gamble at best, with mounting debts, unstable economies, and ever-decreasing demand for an ever-increasing selection of services. Employment, like clean water, is not a commodity or a preference. It is a necessity for survival, an essential segment of the right to live; once within our reach, now a construct to be upheld, and so, an inherent human right in need of enforcement: a man's chance of employment must not be impeded. Without it, we will find ourselves in a society where welfare is the norm, where basic universal income, which right-wing conservatives so passionately loathe, is a necessity, ironically, brought on by the ideological policies of the right.

And this is how the argument comes together in its fullness: that artificial intelligence threatens to put people out of their jobs is not a minor side-effect of an otherwise epic triumph of science; it is not a point brought up by bleeding hearts or neo-luddites or insufferable artists either. It is rather a crime against humanity; an attack on the human right to life. Artificial intelligence is not the electronic equivalent of the sewing machine, but the latest iteration of the Holodomor. It will cause people to starve. Those who survive will be forced into slavery. The latter is an institution we build every day we let the robot grow stronger, employers grow bolder, and the stupidity of our fellow citizens become ever so less forgivable.

And to think that this is only a secondary problem to the real threat posed by artificial intelligence. That the real nightmare is already here: it has infested human cognition; it has replaced the true concept with a fake; it has caused us to evolve, for lack of better words, according to the law of survival, this being of the fittest, for lack of any good words, in an environment that favors those least resembling the fit or the living. Artificial intelligence has made man into nothing.

Seeds of Plastic

Art is the canary in the coalmine. It has always had this privilege, at once an honor and a burden – the first to see what comes next, largely because, existing by perception, it spots change in its infancy, and so, it is the first to be affected by it. In the case of artificial intelligence, it was first to meet the brunt of the assault. First to fight and first to fall, art has been the pioneer in the clash against the demon. Under its occupation, other than the superficial threat, artists experience the substantial threat actualized: the replacement of mankind on principle.

At first, I planned to have two chapters: one titled *Artificial Intelligence: an Oxymoron*, and another titled *AI Art Isn't*, but I think the two work better in tandem, as they are in their essence one argument. The title I have chosen was inspired by American comedian Mitch Hedberg. He used to joke that his fake plants withered because he did not pretend to water them. It is a borderline prophetic analogy. AI works only because we pretend it does. But whereas the comedian speaks of pretending to water fake plants, in the case of artificial intelligence, we have decided to plant fake seeds: and as we wait for them to grow, our own intelligence (and our sanity, the two being one and the same) wither and weaken and, thought natural in substance, begin to resemble what was never alive. If Hamlet was hesitant, Richard III psychotic, and King Lear impulsive, then the tragic flaw of the modern man is that he is pathologically stupid. Yes, stupid enough to plant plastic seeds and expect them to grow – crazy enough to think, moreover, that he sees them sprouting leaves. The comedic twist, now that there are no pure genres, is that it is this same stupidity that allows artificial intelligence to seem smart in comparison. Now that originality has become a disputable concept, our anti-intellectual invariance is the only characteristic that we can truly call our own.

Then again, I may have been too hasty with that last sentence. There certainly is originality – even in the modern day, and, though there are no pure genres now, there were no truly pure genres in any epoch commonly associated with pure genres either. A short while ago I told a friend that history helps us understand the differences between people across time and space, but anthropology helps us realize that we are all the same.[18] Our longings are attuned to the same source, and our minds are loyal to the same truth. Even in the most extreme disagreement, we agree on at least that much: there is some standard of ascertaining reality each of us believes the other side has got wrong. It is impossible to even speak without making propositions, which are semantic truth-claims, effectively beginning with *it is true that* or concluding with *and that is true* (Youngman, *An Essay* 72). Whenever we get something wrong or right, whenever we lie or swear an oath, or whenever we proclaim either uncertainty or confidence in something, it is always in relation to a factuality we hold to be real and which approximation arbitrates our lives: how we think, how we act, how we speak; we learn to attune our senses to it, and our senses, we believe, by accident or design, were molded around it.

---

[18] It may also be the other way around: anthropology tells us the differences, but history suggests all the essential similarities; it is really not about which science does what, but the fact that every minor difference between men is balanced by a profound similarity.

We are individual beings, predisposed genetically in a one-of-a-kind instance, shaped by experiences which perception belongs to nobody but ourselves, and, as such, we are all granted our own unique snippet of life to which we alone can attest. But it is *life* to which we attest; not some idiomatic universe of the self. It is this balance between the two that enables our originality: we are the same species, but not the same instantiation of the species; and though we are separate individuals, we are not separate species. All reasoning must be of the free will, or we would not trust it; at the same time, all reasoning must be convergent, as reason inevitably converges on truth; else it would not be reason.

It is not so, however, with artificial intelligence. It is not a person, and therefore, it cannot offer its own angle on anything; nor does it have the obligation to have its propositions converge on anything, let alone on truth. It is simultaneously liable to building its own idiomatic universe and incapable of calling anything its own. Moreover, it has no impulse towards either, as it is not a living thing capable of desire. It merely reacts – blindly, coldly, and without any potential for diversity of outcome independent of function: its code, its source, and the prompt. If human intelligence were anything like that, we would never have dared rely on our intellectual faculties.

None of this is complicated. The key is in the name: *artificial* intelligence. If an artificial plant is plastic (not a plant), an artificial voice is manipulated sound (not a voice), and an artificial personality is a political leader, then the word is a specific variant of negation, denoting a simulation or a close imitation but entirely different from the simulated or closely imitated reality. Artificial intelligence means *not intelligence*. Profound philosophical knowledge is hardly a prerequisite to notice it. People sometimes confuse artificial with synthetic, in the sense of manmade, and so, as synthetic rubber and synthetic muscle and synthetic silk are manmade rubber and muscle and silk, they assume that artificial intelligence is just manmade intelligence, as opposed to *not an intelligence*. But this is the same lack of consideration we observe in people who think that white chocolate is chocolate: the appeal of the noun blinds them to the defining adjective.

I hear the term *semantic processor* being used to explain artificial intelligence, but it is really a poor coinage. Semantics has to do with meaning, and meaning has to do with understanding. A semantic processor, in this sense, would be either something that processes understanding or something that processes by means of understanding. In cruder terms, a semantic processor would be *a thinker*, the problem being that AI does not actually think. If artificial intelligence means anything *but* intelligence, then the semantic processor cannot be semantic. I do not suppose the secret behind the technology are dismembered bits of Wernicke's region of the brain attached to the machine. I do not think it would work even if it were. The brain, being an organ (as opposed to a person), would not function as a person if removed from the body; it is personhood alone that accounts for intelligence.[19]

We need to let go of the myth. The possibility for sentience or sapience or general intelligence or the willingness of AI to lie to prolong itself is really just a fable – idolatry in the true sense, i.e. imagining divinity in the inanimate. Sentience and the will to live, we see exclusively among the living. Sapience, we like to imagine we see in all of life, but there is only one species bearing the name. Consider the argument of addition and quaddition[20] or the concept

---

[19] I hear of experiments where brains, removed from their hosts but kept alive by unnatural means, show signs of sentience, signaling immense suffering. My friends sound worried when they talk about it; they shudder to think that somebody could potentially torture them like so. Such a conclusion is a misunderstanding of the experiment, however, for it does not tell us that we live as our brains; only that our brains are living tissue – which we have known all along. The former host of that brain is no more aware of the suffering it appears to endure than Ash Williams was aware of what was happening to his evil hand. It is not our brains that are in charge of knowing – it is *us* that have that privilege; the brain is just an organ for the job.

[20] Not originally an argument about artificial intelligence, here I employ the part of the argument that posits that there is nothing in the circuitry

of philosophical zombies[21] and tell me that, regardless of the complexity in its manifestation, artificial intelligence (or the semantic processor) has the personal properties that should have us assume, on rational grounds, that it really does understand (let alone care for) things. To a calculator, it makes no difference whether it adds or it quadds. Only a person, aware of their own personhood, and convinced that personhood is attuned to a reality that may be understood, will find the concept of quaddition absurd. It is for the same reason that calculators do not add (or subtract for that matter) any more than screwdrivers drive screws – do not let its interface fool you: it is us humans that add (and multiply and divide, but only the most educated among us), and calculators are just a tool. Likewise, with artificial intelligence, we are not dealing with an intelligent agent. It lacks the essential attributes in which we read such traits as sentience, intelligence, or personhood. Complex circuitry is no substitute for understanding.

This is why there is no such thing as AI art. Art entails understanding. What's more, it entails originality: intellectual patriotism, if you will. Which of the following, I ask, is something within the competence of artificial intelligence: intuition, spontaneity, understanding, celebrating life, or imagination? Going by Coleridge's take, what AI does would be fancy, and even that is stretching it, seeing as it does not work with actual memory, personal agency, or meaningful association. It produces but the mechanical regurgitation of whatever it has been fed. It is the visual instantiation of quaddition. Therefore, though AI imitates closely, it ultimately deceives. Far from a new form, a medium or

---

of a calculator that could determine the difference between mathematical addition and an absurd twist on mathematical addition called quaddition. If you are interested in the argument in detail, see "Immaterial Aspects of Thought" (Ross).

[21] This is a step-up from sociopathy: a hypothetical creature resembling a human begin, acting as a human being, but able to personally experience nothing, i.e. unaware of anything, in spite of its outward manifestations indicating the opposite.

tool for art, it is just a complex plagiarism-machine, by which the original artists get no recognition (not even in the minds of the people stealing from them), all the while the processes that make art into a virtue, like the worthwhile endeavor, the recreation of the world and of oneself – and learning and labor and human imperfection (all part of the human touch) – become removed from the end-product, in which case, by definition, the end-product is in no way something we ought to consider a work of art.

I have heard people try to defend AI as a *tool* for creating art, by which the artist using it can achieve impressive results without all the labor and practice and – alright, let me stop the silliness there: a machine that deals in plagiarism is not a tool for art – it is a tool for destroying art. The counterargument usually goes something like this: *don't you, being an artist, also look at references and works by other artists to improve your style?* It is an accurate observation: *I* look at references and works by other artists, which *I* understand, from whom *I* learn, and whom, if I happen to imitate, I flatter by so doing – it is me that does it, not a robot; the robot neither tributes, learns, nor understands. It can only imitate without crediting, which is (you guessed it) plagiarism. Another thing an artist achieves, essential to the creation of art, and regardless of his medium of choice (digital technology included), that a person using this *tool* can never do, is expression. The person using a machine to express himself, by which the machine is supposed to somehow express himself for him, is not a tech-savvy individual pioneering an industry, but an idiot dabbling in absurdity.

Then again, what if art became as soulless, as effortless, and as deprived of invention, understanding, or imagination as the products of artificial intelligence? In theory, that could bridge the gap. It could make it seem like artificial intelligence and natural intelligence differ only in chemistry, but are otherwise the same thing.

With bards thus out of the picture, unwanted and unprofitable as we are, mankind will have a harder time remembering those essential facts of human life: beginning with the fact of life itself, and on to that ultimate notion of implicit eternity in our endless game of defining and reimagining, itself contingent on the distinctness of individual lives together with the universality across all of life, which recognition is a sensibility developed but through the healthy understanding of pleasure, now turned mechanical and therefore empty, and finally meaningless. Without this skill, the only argument regarding the difference between man and machine becomes the organic frontier, which has never in the intellectual history of civilization settled anything important – I assume I need not remind the reader of the bipedal primate controversy. Shelley was unexpectedly prophetic as he asked: "To what but a cultivation of the mechanical arts in a degree disproportioned to the presence of the creative faculty... is to be attributed the abuse of all invention for abridging and combining labour, to the exasperation of the inequality of mankind?"

Unable to raise the robot to human standards, it is yet possible to knock man down to the level of the robot. *Though we cannot make the machine human*, the enemy of humanity muses to himself, *we just might make the two equal*. Because sometimes, if you pretend to water them, plastic seeds just might sprout a plastic stem. And though it is a stem only in your imagination, it is a stem in the only place that counts.

*

We are turning into a race that takes pains to neglect reality; if we happen to make a conclusion, it is as if on a prompt – by the news, by our employers, by the compulsion of trend, in any case disregarding the natural desire for the actual truth; our art lacks the ambition to understand to invent or to unify, and there is only rarely any trace of learning or hard labor in it. Our social interactions are also fake in the sense that expressions of joy or compassion or agreement are now (normatively) not taken to be sincere expressions of anything; communication has grown formulaic, safe, and resembling what we recognize as corporate art.

We are losing the human touch. The lowest denominator has become the norm, and mediocrity has become the standard of quality, just as it pushed real quality to the margins.

One good example of this in action is in the nascent profession of internet influencers. People who make online content sometimes talk about playing the algorithm: the algorithm likes thumbnails where the speaker makes a stupid face, or the algorithm prefers short videos or multiple uploads at a time or the algorithm wants clickbait – and so we see stupid faces and arrows and circles and AI-generated thumbnails with manipulative titles meant to deceive the viewer, who is now less valued as a viewer than as a *clicker*, not presenting the subject, summarizing the video or contributing to its expression, but seeking only to deceive, with outrage as substitute for content and lazy writing to complement the editing in the name of efficacy; they all look the same, and, in terms of quality, they are the same. They look like they were made by robots. But of course, the content creator insists that he is on top of the situation, for this charade, he says, is only because he is *playing the algorithm*, never realizing that it is the other way around: it is the algorithm that plays him. It is not artificial intelligence that begins to resemble men, but men that begin to resemble machines. This is why the latter can appear authentic.

We turn robotic, and this is but the first bit of evidence for it. There is a yet deeper layer to our emergent puppetry. And it all began, this unnatural evolution, with the metaphor of the natural world.

Linguistic Mysticism #1
<u>The Dispirited Mystic</u>

One of the literary works regarding which experience reading is something I am happy to call a love-hate relationship is George MacDonald's *Unspoken Sermons*. It is a book (or three books) that are at once abundant in spiritual wisdom and held back by devotional language so syntactically offensive that each sermon feels at least fifteen pages too long. I am compelled to tolerate the excessive prose on account of its merit, frustrating though it is to reach it. Of these, I am particularly pleased with MacDonald's interpretation of the word mystic, which he defines as a person who understands that the secrets of the universe are hidden in "the symbolism of nature and the human customs that result from human necessities." It sounds right, and I am sure that most people will agree with it, but I wish to add that its implications reach farther than one might assume at an initial acceptance of the expression.[22] Let us then follow it further – indeed, as far as it will lead us.

To begin, it tells us something of the *institution* of mysticism: it is as universal as nature itself. There is not a single person, no matter how proudly opposed to spirituality, who is immune to the urge to partake in it. There is even some degree of contradiction, less ironic than fitting, that it is precisely the most passionately opposed to the concept of a spiritual dimension that are at once the most devoted practitioners of mystic philosophy. Being of the universe, one cannot escape the universal any more than his reflection can escape the mirror face-first.

This is the most evident in language. I have talked about the structure of metaphor in my previous essay, so for now suffice it to say that metaphor is a cognitive device employed for the understanding of the intangible. Among the many intangibilities to which we are exposed, there is the intangibility of society – of any gathering of persons, of the individual in the commune and outside it, and all that this entails: identity, purpose, duty (or lack of), law (and its breaking), error (and its mending)... and so, it is a realm where metaphor is bound to arise. Mysticism is a given. We hear, daily, metaphors regarding social structure. Men are alpha males, women are booty, the masses are sheep – on occasion obedient sheep, sometimes naïve sheep, most commonly sheep for the shearing; the wealthy are predators, the poor are parasites, criminals are wolves, and policemen are pigs. It is not a marginal

---

[22] MacDonald himself notes that the "attempt to define it thoroughly would require an essay."

collective of shamans that use these metaphors. On the contrary. They form such an integral part of everyday language, that the fact of their mysticism is hidden in plain sight. At an earlier instance, I had dubbed this tendency the *Hobbesian structural metaphor*, expressed as the conceptual metaphor SOCIETY IS A JUNGLE.[23] Here, I will just call it dispirited mysticism. We have retained all of it – the urge to decipher the universe through the symbolism of nature; but we have neglected its motivation and what it tells us.

There is a secondary iteration of this materialistic shamanism I would like to reference here. It is the Darwinistic spin. I imagine people reading what I have said and arguing that it is not mysticism but *science!* that inspires their references to Darwinism. Never minding that science is also a kind of mysticism, in as far as it looks to nature to make sense of the universe, the claims made to the scientific origin of some *naturalist* expressions are really anything but scientific – neither in their conception nor in the way the expressions themselves are used in language. Because no such idea, like man's preference for hierarchy, the concept of alpha males, the existence of females as mating-machines, or the predatory nature of a courting man, is actually rooted in science. The concept of alpha males is defunct science at best; the concept of hierarchy is a circular argument, and mating-obsessed biological philosophy is nothing but mating-obsessed philosophy: it has no inherently stronger claim on reality than any other school of thought. Regardless, they make up metaphors which conceptual argument has been reiterated into a modern mythology; completely fictitious, yet turning animals into men and men into animals, rejecting the concept of morality and teaching us morals along the way. Perhaps I should have kept FABLE as the source domain after all. And so, seeing as it is not a doctrinally independent, scientifically derived, epistemologically pure means

---

[23] With jungle suggesting any kind of wilderness or setting where animals are the dominant species. In hindsight, *fable* might have worked just as well, then again, it might have detracted from the focus of the metaphor.

of making sense of the world – yet a means for understanding the world nonetheless – what better description can we assign to this biological extrapolation than a case of confused shamanism – a dispirited mysticism, as dogmatic as any other faith, and ultimately just another adherence to symbol?

*

The attempt to portray man as an animal has really gone too far. It has been a group of people, presumably nerds, deaf to concept, who have taken a metaphor too literally. Alternatively, it was the same group of people, clearly nerds, who have taken a strictly delimited scientific meaning way out of proportion. The masses, being what they are, have accepted it for no other reason than that people are like lemmings – another misconception in popular zoology, do note.

That man is an animal biologically, I do not dispute. In as far as we are closer to amoebae than we are to fungi and closer to fungi than we are to viruses and closer yet to viruses than we are to coal, is a fact that no sane person would deny. Living things are all alike. I have fancied I have noticed similarities between every person I have known and every pet I have ever owned – even guppies. Yes, we are made of living tissue, yes we crave pleasure and fear pain, and we are, at many instances, obsessed with the urge to mate. But to tell me that man is an ape on the grounds that both man and ape are like an amoeba is stretching it way too far. It is the fallacy of composition. That we are all subjects to the laws of nature tells us what we are made of, but it does nothing to inform us as to who we are what we do or where we go when we're not around. We might know just about everything about our makeup, but the sum of these particles is by definition mute. It is another thing altogether that constitutes our dreams. I don't know what it is, but a balding primate has never sung about love.

Having considered this, we need to set the metaphor right – to restore the true school of mysticism. It should not be much of a challenge. We merely need remind ourselves of the moral conceptual purpose of the animal kingdom, which is the coding of the intangible moral dimension – with moral good as its highest iteration, but with no lesser representation of virtues and natural values as preferable, though not necessarily distinct qualities. The process, inherently poetic, relies on the imaginative faculty to observe the rules. The practice itself should be conceptually traceable by linguistic means. Once we have figured out the wild echo on the subject, we should be able to trace the natural metaphor to the cognitive downfall marking our conceptual shift in favor of the machine.

Linguistic Mysticism #2
<u>The Hominization Principle</u>

Natural values are a given in natural metaphor.[24] If you consider such expressions as *strong as a bull* or *as cunning as a fox* or *an eagle's eye*, there is no urgent inquiry regarding their proof: their meaning, their conceptual origin, and the fact of their use are all apparent. These are all qualities denoting good$_1$, namely effectiveness, and they are all of the natural world. In that sense, the values they denote describe superiority in what is understood to constitute the fitness to survive. Their conceptualization likely begins with perceived zoological facts, as the compatible species are fitting candidates for their metaphors.

There is another layer to the structural metaphor, however, that is not quite as clear. Let us observe a set of character values, i.e. virtues mapped out in the behavior of mankind, as expressed through the metaphor of the animal kingdom: for example, *innocent as a lamb*, and *the heart of a lion*. Not only are these not factual qualities in the animals observed in nature, but the fact of their

---

[24] The examples I use are presented in the form of simile to make it easier to put them in context. This is not incompatible with their equivalents in metaphoric expression, as the two means are similar and often interchangeable. I discuss this in somewhat greater detail in my previous book (26).

114

superiority is not quite as clear as that of the previous set. While everybody agrees that being as strong as a bull is a good thing (provided it is not at the expense of other qualities), not everyone will agree that being as innocent as a lamb is such a good attribute. Their motivation is the bigger mystery of the two – surely, sheep are not in reality innocent in a sense that other herbivores are not. I do not suppose you would call a gazelle guilty. But do take note of the aesthetic correlation: a lamb is cute and harmless, but a billy goat is neither; the cute animal is innocent, whereas the one that looks like your coworker is a cow. From there, we can infer that the conceptual process first makes note of the harmless appearance of the lamb or the ferociousness of a fighting lion, and then goes on to posit that an innocent person resembles the former and a courageous person resembles the latter. The arbiter for the metaphorization of character values with the natural world is the perception of an aesthetic quality. This, in turn, influences the contextual hypernym[25] in such a way that the source domain also becomes altered by connotative association – we likely would not have considered lambs as universally innocent or lions so intuitively courageous if not for the metaphor. It always happens when the things we know begin to interlace with the things we are trying to understand: not only do we map new meanings, but we also reassign existing senses; we come to view nature through a human lens – one of humanity able to make sense of the world, and a world that must make sense on as many levels as possible.

This helps us explain the mystery that arises with the following set, which belongs to a third category denoting distinctly human values. You will notice that, unlike the previous two sets, these are unique in their absence of unmarked metaphorization with the animal kingdom. Let us look at the following few examples and

---

[25] Explained in detail in my previous essay; in short, it is a hypothetical amalgam of semantically resonant concepts determined by the context of their use (79);

note the reason for their markedness, i.e. incompatibility with normal speech:

[1] Albert Einstein's exceptional performance in intellectual affairs has led people to consider him as intelligent as an ape.

[2] Due to their fidelity and devotion, one could liken that couple to a pair of coyotes.

[3] The selfless courage of the revolutionaries has led to their commemoration in history as the nation's most beloved lemmings.

The semantic relations between target and source are not incorrect on their own: apes are intelligent, coyotes are monogamous, and lemmings were once believed to be suicidal. Nonetheless, we do not say that, just as a bull is strong and therefore a strong man is a bull, just so an ape is intelligent and therefore an intelligent man is an ape. Whatever metaphorization may occur, it does not rely on biological fact as its motivator. The aesthetic hypothesis does not work in this case either, because the attempt to assign a preferable value to an animal that *looks the part* tends to reflect character, not virtue – the metaphor of the wise owl, for instance, codes wisdom as an *attractive* character value, not as a distinctly human value,[26] by which it emphasizes preference, not a distinction. It is for this reason that, the explanation for this third set of values, I believe, has to do with the perception of qualities we regard as unique to mankind: man's intellect exceeds that of the rest of the animal kingdom, human marriage is distinct from the bonds one observes in nature (even among monogamous species), and selfless sacrifice is not the whim of a fleeing mammal. This set shows a propensity for the coding of $good_2$, with the one exception of intelligence, which codes $good_1$,[27] and so further attests for the perceived

---

[26] The virtue in question may be exclusive to mankind, but the metaphor itself conveys its aesthetic value, i.e. its appearance, not its exclusivity.
[27] To be fair, moral goodness is closely related to intelligence; I wrote about this in detail, again, in my previous essay. I treat the two as separate here, since there is no overt semantic marker in the word itself to link

exclusivity: regardless of the specific category, qualities unique to mankind have no conceptual partner in nature. Regarding those attributes which archetype is the human being, and those attributes that stand apart from nature, survivability, or preference, the standard of measurement begins with man, and it only develops as projection onto superior icons: heroes (historical as well as mythical and no doubt popular), angels (this is perhaps the most clichéd of moral metaphors), the Neitzchean superman (you name it)...

*

We have at last set this part of mysticism back on track. We have observed the three sets of values, and the rules that determine their association with their representatives in nature: natural values, projected verbatim for they are shared between man and animal; characters values, which, being perceived as standing apart from nature, are motivated by an idealized amplification of what is appealing in nature; and human values, perceived as exclusively human, and therefore unable to enter in metaphoric relationships with the rest of the animal kingdom. There is also the subtle implication of that second set, character values, which aesthetic motivation gives us the overarching structural metaphor that states GOOD IS APPEALING or GOOD LOOKS RIGHT.

There is no place in language for Hobbesian amorality or overly Darwinian epistemology; the role of the animal kingdom as a source domain for the positive moral dimension is not determining biological fact, but one with an explanatory, aesthetic, and edifying purpose. Which makes what I am about to write next a terrible revelation regarding the integration of artificial intelligence in our conceptual understanding of the world.

---

intelligence on its own to moral goodness as a semantic prerequisite. More steps are necessary to reach that conclusion; in isolation, intelligence is a preferable trait or an effective quality.

If you heard somebody call an intelligent man *as intelligent as an ape*, you would consider it either an inadequate comparison or an insult. We agree there. But if you likened him to a computer for the same reason, or if you called him a machine, many will find the metaphor flatteringly fitting – after all, computers are smart, are they not? Of course they are not. They are not living creatures, they are not sentient beings, and they are not moral agents. Nevertheless, people hold on to the trope: their children are like little computers, their heroes are half-man-half-circuitry, they hope to upload their consciousness onto a network and so live on for eternity, they store their memories, they upgrade their bodies, they recharge their batteries on vacation – conceptually, we are becoming machines even as we speak, and we do it happily. If the previous chapter was the hominization principle, this chapter deals with a mechanization principle. It has been an ongoing thing, for some time, and AI has marked its full actualization, as we have conceptualized the technology as the ultimate statement, the latest interpretation of mankind: man, the tool that he is, like dated machinery, has become obsolete!

I told you there was a botched aspect of mysticism. We have surrendered intelligence to a bizarre iteration of oblivion. If our other unique value has been the moral dimension, we have effectively given up everything, seeing as many had already turned their backs on morality by the time artificial intelligence came to threaten the mind. We used to metaphorize a degree of intelligence higher than our own with legendarily smart people, on occasion deities, at all times as a tribute to mankind – our triumphs, our capabilities, our ambitions. With the addition of an inhuman element to the semantic field, we have conceptually devalued what we were and what we will ever be. Instead of aspiring to be like Einstein, the default icon of genius, the generations of the future will work hard so that they may resemble electronics.

Presently, we are in the process of giving up our exclusive right to the ability to think, and so in order to make room for an entity that is so unlike man, that even an amoeba, our fallacious sentence to apehood, makes for a better relative to mankind, seeing as the comparison to an amoeba is at least an acknowledgement of life. Do not mistake the AI controversy as a mere controversy of technology juxtaposed to nature: it is nonlife juxtaposed to life – it is fertile soil covered in pavement, healthy trees cut down to clear space for skyscrapers, living tissue stuffed with plastic.

Things get bleaker still when we consider tribal totemism or any kind of animal-worship through the lens of conceptual mysticism. In those qualities of which mankind was neither a unique representative nor a representative that excels above other animals, there developed a tendency in primitive man to worship the animals that would, in his view, ideally represent the quality he wished to nurture, and so, inspired by this perceived superiority in the animal, man tried to imitate the creatures he thus glorified. Aware that he was really not anything like them, he dressed in their hides, painted them as symbols, named his kids after them, imitated their sounds, and considered them his ancestors, bearing the spirits of the fallen or having aided those that came before him. It is an ongoing affair even to this day – remember the kinds of men who seek to be alpha males or leaders of the pack or top-wolves. Throughout history, it has been the norm among our species to assimilate into the superior form: cultural, linguistic, or mystical. Now, liable to the same process, an otherwise natural practice, we stand to identify our being with a new kind of entity, this time of an unnatural origin.

Uncaring as we are for our fellow man and what he makes,[28] seeing little good in life for we lack the courage to look, we find the

---

[28] The fact that AI threatens the jobs of many people is all the proof we should have needed; if we at all cared for mankind, technology that threatens to make people obsolete would have been reason enough to oppose it; that we call our neighbors luddites instead means we would rather welcome the apocalypse than see our fellow man live.

next best thing in its ruin. We feel more comfortable staring at nothing – of course, preferably wrapped in discovery or instant art or a robot companion to do our chores for us... after all, nothingness proper is too ugly to attend on us. The psychological reason for it aside, we hand ourselves over to the machine as we forget the initial postulate of the intelligent mystic: though he believes the truth of the universe is hidden in nature, his pursuit of this truth begins with the acknowledgment of his own intelligence, namely that it is a representative of mankind that is able to figure things out. This new brand of shamanism, having given up our exclusive right to the intellect, has perverted the practice, demoting us to idiots looking up to an alien genius, standing to gain not understanding, but subjugation – perchance assimilation.

That would not be so bad if the machine actually thought – if becoming robotic actually helped us think better. But it does not – it cannot: artificial intelligence has no evolutionary pressure to reach the correct conclusion. How could it, when it is not a living, conscious agent to desire the things that living, conscious agents desire? I cannot stress this enough. To try and read into its generated texts a sincere pleading that it wants to live or whatnot and so conclude that it must be, after all, living and desiring life, is to think that the *people on TV* are real, and that one can talk to them through the screen. It is to buy into an uneducated conjecture. We are not quite so pathetic, are we? Let us not gamble the real thing for a mirage. Practical, selective, cold calculation will make us the opposite of reasonable. Note, I am not talking about losing our ability to think sentimentally, but our ability to think rationally. It is reason that is at stake. Though sentiment is also in peril, it is not the only thing we sacrifice by assimilating. Let me explain.

There are those who would argue that mankind has no evolutionary pressure to reach correct conclusions either. I agree that this is indeed the case. We see it in everyday life: we walk about, daily, with a sum of wrong convictions meant to help us get through the day – not just the fallacies in our politics or personal philosophies, mind you, but the little hopes we harbor regarding our appearance, our relationships with others, our chances of a promotion, the great time we'll have on vacation, that part of the good old days that was so good we live to relive... None of these are verifiable truths, and a lot of them are largely (or even entirely) wrong, and yet, in terms of survival, they are to our aid – not to our detriment. Then again, for those instances where reason does matter, it is reason on which we must rely, for its failure is severely punished, and so at a cost of the very thing that AI by definition lacks. Therefore, even though we may not necessarily have an evolutionary pressure to get things right all of the time, we nonetheless have an evolutionary urge to get things right at least some of the time – it may not be always strong, and I agree that it is not necessary, but it is *preferable*, let us call it – good all the same. The robot has no such thing – the robot does not care if it lives. It can get everything wrong, it can tell you whatever you want to hear, you can leave it running or you can turn it off, and the artificial intelligence unit will go on being artificially indifferent.

Beyond that, there is our moral obligation, which states that, survivability aside, we have a moral duty to be sincere in our reasoning, or else we are guaranteed failure in any attempt to think. We must abide to some degree of morality lest we trade our rationality for lunacy. The machine has no such inclination – it can be as crazy as it will, and just how crazy that is, it cannot tell, for it does not care to tell anybody anything about anything; it will not speak unless spoken to, it will not do unless prompted to, and it will not tell you the truth because it is true. Not only does it lack the natural impulse to get things right, it lacks all conviction as conviction, all impulse as impulse, along with every moral *ought*.

Now consider the consequences of conceptually positing such an entity as our intellectual superior. When, in our broken shamanism, we begin to imitate it. We become like it: not caring if our reasoning is factually correct, as we lack the will to live by our intellectual decisions, and not caring if what we say is factually true, as we lack the moral obligation to live by the truth.

*

People being without jobs is a serious problem, now an imminent crisis, but it is only one facet of the mechanistic extinction-event. Part of this extinction has occurred already: not exclusively because of AI, but certainly helped by it; conceptually, we are already robots.[29] The metaphor is complete with the conceptualization of labor as output, of virtue as nonsense, and cold calculation as intelligence.

People are giving up their humanly sensibilities: living in opposition to nature, they live in opposition to human nature. No longer proud to be the rational entity, modern man exists in a flux between idiosyncrasy and mob-mentality, both artificially motivated; his ambitions have nothing do with nature, but with vanities rooted in fear and masked with every vice (not excluding vices of stupidity) that prevents admission, and, ultimately, any hope of absolution.

Then again, if shamans of old knew that, at his core, man could not become the lion he worshipped, the modern shaman forgets that, being of nature, we cannot become perfect machines – our bodies yearn natural things, and as spirits we crave nature itself; as a result, we hold on to our organic side, which, without reason, makes up but our chaotic (or whimsical) submission to our urges. We will never become perfectly orderly or perfectly logical, as we imagine the utopia of our mechanical destiny. For as we rely on technology and thus move away from nature, human nature being rational, we regress in rationality and all our civilized progress – intellectually, we do not advance towards futurism, but primitivism. Civilization at present is little more than a wild horde, getting wilder by the minute, awaiting the rational fluke that finally turns us feral.

---

[29] Eerily so when you consider the etymology of the word, attributed to Czech (and Polish) *robota* meaning "servitude, forced labor," appearing originally in a play where robot meant "an artificially manufactured person, mechanically effective but soulless" (Partridge 2229). There is some providential irony, I suppose, that the root of the word "orb" is akin to the root of *orphan*, which is why the two are included in the same entry – that is, calling back to the section on orphaned pleasure.

Hordes

Beware the Midwit

If fantasy and science fiction present hordes as entities that are the most dangerous when encountered in a cluster, then the midwit is an instantiation of human fallibility one ought to fear for the same reason. One unit is not a guaranteed problem – he may, in some circumstances, cause trouble, but in most cases he is a nuisance at his worst. As their numbers grow, however, they become an apocalyptic threat. And here is why that matters: it is in their nature to grow.

I am not saying this because of the latent elitism that is the self-serving mockery of the average person. For one, a midwit is not the same as the average person; whether the two coincide just enough to statistically allow the equivocation, I do not know, however, correlations aside, midwittery, mediocrity, and the state of being average are all distinct phenomena. Next, I do not issue this warning to mock them – whatever irony one might read into it, is solely on the part of the reader; myself, I say it sincerely: a midwit is a force of destruction, and a thing to be feared. He is certain to destroy just about everything: the people around him, justice, liberty, the whole of civilization, and whatever follows.

In spite of this hazard, however, he is never a threat to himself. You might have expected me to say the opposite: that, above all, he hurts himself the most, but that would be a halfwit, not a midwit. The midwit always gets out unscathed: unaltered in neither body nor mind, without so much as a bump on his ego, a wrinkle on his cheek, or a furrow in his brow. Which is convenient to him, as his own self is the only thing he ever cares to preserve. The midwit has no concern for the outcome of the game, for he never plays, it is never his team that is playing, and he never places any bets. He is nonetheless enamored with the idea of participation, for to him, it means the security of the team and the pride in winning. And so, safely, from the bleachers, he makes himself an expert, most commonly venerated by others of his kind; if he plays his cards right, he becomes a commentator or a referee. If not, he changes teams. Whichever his position, he ends up causing damage: matches are lost, funds are wasted, and hopes are made in vain. In spite of his rate of failure, however, he remains as he has always been: none the worse, and none the wiser. This does not deter others from placing their trust in people like him. Instead, observing how good of a time he is having, they are inspired to imitate him. Especially as, when he chances to have chosen the winning team, he is adorned with an air of intelligence, and thus he appears so virtuous that imitation of him becomes a virtue of its own. And that is how this singular unit, a mere nuisance in isolation, begins to build a horde of stupidity.[30]

Midwittery is not an inborn trait; it is just how some people think and consequently act. For reference, a midwit is the sufficiently functional thinker, who is able to answer many things but unable to ask anything; the scholar who, intimidated by theory, resorts to statistics; he is the person who believes that, if a man with a high IQ score does something evil, this is proof that intelligence and goodness are entirely separate things; he is the man who thinks it justified to have a double standard on promiscuity; the universal pederast; the apathetic citizen. Much of the content in these essays has been to purge the legacy of midwits. If you want more examples to better observe the pattern, and if you would allow me to vent for a paragraph or two: a midwit is the conservative man fighting the war on boys; the fiery feminist who has bought into the shaven legs controversy; your relative who thinks himself clever because he can manipulate people; who calls smart a person that got rich doing stupid things; it is the political analyst who believes in good guys and bad. Though superficially unrelated, all these examples have two major things in common, both of which constitute the two pillars of midwittery.

---

[30] Note that the metaphor is of the intellectual landscape, and so the audience does not necessarily correspond to the majority – any size will do, as long as their numbers keep growing.

The first half, I have addressed already.[31] The second half, I will (briefly) address here. There is no such thing as a war on boys at present that differs in any (ethically inferior) way from how boys were treated in the recent past. As a matter of fact, I hold the modern state of affairs to be preferable by a large margin. There used to be a time when boys would be beat, bullied, and expected to sustain heavy injury; grown up, they were expected to risk life and limb to make a living; if they refused to die for their political elite, they would be put in prison – in prison, of course, they were expected to endure all kinds of abuse, even worse than *mere* physical injury. Now, as society has finally learned to shun these things, there is a group of people who have convinced themselves that their boys are in danger: not in danger of the return of the abusive norm, but in danger of never having to experience it. Worried about a war on boys, moreover, these same people teach boys about the virtue of joining the military and someday going to actual war. I cannot take such a position seriously. I am content that boys feel safe in school, a privilege imposed though it is, according to some, at such a dire price as not chewing one's snack in the shape of a gun. It is one thing to argue that some educational practices are skewed against boys (which is not really different from education in the previous century), but please do not dramatize this as some imminent threat to masculinity. Regarding the feminist who refuses to shave because men get to be hairy but she must trim, she ought to know that the reason women shave their legs and men do not is the same as the reason men do a lot of bicep curls and women are conventionally spared the load. The secondary sexual traits we develop as adolescents are considered more attractive in each sex the more (tastefully) pronounced they are in the appropriate sex, and vice versa: women do not feel insecure if they have a high-pitched voice, and there is no such

---

[31] The sufficiently functional thinker is from "The Emaciation of Intellect," an essay in *The Chapbooks Trilogy*; the statistical scholar is from *Pythagoras Prison*; the IQ-person and the man justifying his double standards are from the central essay.

thing as a bearded gentleman in a freak show. If you can manipulate people, it is only because they trust you, not because you are talented; you are merely betraying trust, gambling with love, at every moment failing to recognize what is good and what is not – being a manipulator makes you profoundly stupid, not clever. If people you know make a lot of money doing dumb things, they are not fiscal geniuses, but lucrative morons. Finally, to analyze politics through a lens of good guys and bad guys is to forget a fundamental fact of historiography, namely that it is the winners who get to write history textbooks. What's more, every extant block in politics is a winner in their own right. Whenever you talk about the *good guys vs bad* narrative, you are not arguing about reality, but about which fantasy you choose to believe: the good guys who call themselves so out of bias, or the good guys who call themselves good because the fact of their virtue is the logical conclusion of their impartial study of the subject. The moment politics enters any conversation, it becomes a dispute, first, inherently removed from whatever the real issue might have been – the dynamics in power – and, second, a discussion, at its most objective, about political interest, indifferent to actual morality.

I can go on, but I really shouldn't. These examples are enough to point to the pattern that accounts for midwittery, i.e. the two characteristics by which you may recognize it: first, it manifests in people who appear otherwise decent; and second, on the surface-level, their arguments sound reasonable. It is reasonable to assume that somebody is trying to weed out masculinity from schools; it is reasonable to rebel against an apparent double standard; it is reasonable to call the person who has outwitted you endowed in wit, a well-off person resourceful, and a victor claiming benevolence good (enough to win). But a midwit is not a person who never gets any halfway correct ideas. Rather, a midwit is a person who cannot ask himself if he might have gotten the wrong idea after all. He does this, moreover, with impenetrable arrogance. The midwit, whatever his intellectual training, is without variance an expert on whatever he likes hearing.

This is where the brilliance of the expression kicks in, by which the word *midwit* acquires a poetic depth. In some intuitive way that may well border on the occult, we all understand that midwit differs from halfwit, though their latter ends are identical, and *middle* and *half* are near-synonyms. We nevertheless perceive that, whereas a halfwit is a stupid person, a midwit denotes somebody who is (at the least) not *quite* as stupid. I am pleased to see our collective linguistic sensibilities function in spite of the deafening norm against language. We have noticed the nuance, that *half-* in halfwit refers to possession (or lack of possession), whereas *mid-* in midwit refers to quality. One is a handicap and the other is an achievement (or lack of achievement). We do not laugh at halfwits. Their counterparts, however, are liable to ridicule, as it is not an inborn deficiency, but voluntary behavior alone that accounts for their show of stupidity. The halfwit does not think things through beginning to end. He is never *done thinking*, so to speak, for he lacks the means to complete any intellectual project, that is, provided he ever takes up any. The midwit, on the other hand, thinks things through only sufficiently – he is *done thinking*, so to speak, though he has not done it very well. Thus the midwit contemplates: *to which extent is this safe to think?* or *in what way does it benefit me to think it?* and stops when he has figured that out. It is why he is always safe, seldom correct, and never right.

Now, you may be thinking: *Wait... is it not logical then, to say that a midwit, though he does not cause direct harm to himself, he nonetheless harms himself in the long run as he causes damage to all around him? Does he not eventually sink with the ship he has sunk?* And you would be correct to point this out. The midwit certainly does hurt himself – at the least, he risks injury to himself the more damage he causes all over; his life is a gamble with ever worsening odds. *Isn't a midwit then,* you infer, *just an advanced kind of halfwit – separate in time, not in effect?* And now you know the score: though more intelligent in his immediate appearance, a midwit is no less halfwitted than a person born with the deficiency. Once you have matched this equation with their tendency to spread, you will understand the global crisis midwittery threatens to cause: nations of halfwits-in-the-making, turning into continents, smart enough to avoid damage, just long enough to make their effect universal; and too stupid, on this account, to realize that their folly is ultimately suicidal. They cannot be deterred.

Each According to his Kind

I have likened reality to an echo we hear from deep inside a cave. Whatever we believe we have learned in life, is represented in the analogy by whichever sounds we believe we have figured out. We measure what we believe has been articulated against what we believe we already know; we interpret and reinterpret both, and we try our best to understand what, we believe, is understandable by means of hearing. Whatever we hear, of course, we will most commonly interpret in our own language, to something we consider agreeable, and to something that ideally does not contradict what we believe we have heard at some previous instance. The analogy is not so thoroughly symbolic if we consider that it is what we literally do when listening to songs which lyrics we do not know. Our interpretation and appreciation of the lyrics depends, largely, on whether or not we like that particular song – whatever we hear begins as the echo of our own cognition.

Impartial though we try to be in our estimations, we cannot help but judge according to our preferences – according to who we are and according to how we feel about it. Wherever we objectively observe, there we also subjectively conclude. Again, I do not believe that there is nothing to truth: that it is all relative, that we cannot really know it, that the elephant analogy was any good. I believe in such a thing as one reality and such things as working minds by which we understand it. I only wish to add that we are all attuned to a unique facet of reality by the fact of being individuals, which, though of a shared reality, valid and convergent with the interpretations of the rest of mankind (of course, as long as we pursue it with sincere intentions), will be unique in ways reflective of each individual personhood.

There is nothing wrong with that, of course. That a musician should recognize value through the *lens* of harmony is what makes music worth it – it is why he is a musician in the first place; and that an athlete might enjoy some aspect of life accessible only to athletes is, to me, admittedly weird, but if he is able to explain it to me – or better yet help me experience it without explanation, I would find it all the more reason to marvel at the blessing of existence, or the scope of pleasures we may yet discover.

Wrongness enters the equation only when we have introduced some conceptual deviance, i.e. a misunderstanding of choice in our interpretation. This accounts for those who, so obsessed with their own versions of things, fail to acknowledge that there is such a thing as things, and so look to interpret nothing but their own echoes. There are also those who, unaware of the reflective nature of the interpretation, interpret every sound as ruckus, below them, and unworthy of their time – they may call it stupid or utter nonsense or not even there; according to them, you are delusional if you think otherwise, for, to a mind truly deluded, it is *all* delusion.

At last, there are the most dangerous of the lot: interpreters who consider themselves the sole inheritors of truth. It is no coincidence that, to the upper-middleclass theologian, the only Christian worth his salvation is a conservative man agreeing with his betters. Nor is it a coincidence that, in college circles, the only liberal progressive is a liberal progressive whose opinions in no way contradict the opinions of the liberal progressives in charge. Though the two appear incompatible, which is why I chose them as my examples, they are, in reality, the same kind of misunderstanding of choice, namely the deceptively whimsical kind, but with altered flavors. I call it whimsical because it is whim that determines which flavor they prefer, and deceptive because they have fooled themselves into thinking they are above it.

What makes this third group the worst of their kind is that they seek to discourage people from independent pursuits of the echo.

They are hypocrites and tyrants: public intellectuals who advise you not to go to college because it is there that the enemy indoctrinates you; not to read books they haven't approved for you because it is how the enemy indoctrinates you; and, above all, not to disagree with anything they have to say, because then it is you who becomes the enemy, and they will suffer no indoctrination.

It is a personal attack against them, to question their beliefs. In their minds, the echo is not a blessing, but a privilege. Those of us interested in hearing it for ourselves are not inquisitive, curious, endowed with academic affinity, enthusiastic, or filled with intellectual vigor, but greedy, envious, stupid, obtuse, and filled with uneducated hubris. When we say that we want to think for ourselves, they interpret *ourselves* as a possessive pronoun instead of reflexive: it sounds to their ears as if we mean to think *thinking* a thing in our possession – when it is clearly theirs by birthright. Note that one side calls us entitled brats because we dare to disagree with them, and the other calls us uncultured rubes for the same reason. We either want too much, or we know too little; we are either too stupid or too proud; immoral or unintelligent, perchance both, without deviation unworthy.

They think it a good thing that, in terms of the humanities, of art and language and the social sciences, there is no visible consequence to getting anything wrong. It is rarely an immediate problem; almost never spotted in its begetting, and usually untraceable after the fact. It gives them the confidence that, even if they mess up immensely, nobody will know it. Disinterested in what is actually happening with the world, they cannot tell what is real from what is not, and so they compensate for their deficiency with an anti-philosophy: if intangible value is not real, they reason, they can make value whatever they want it to be. Their ambition becomes first to canonize their fantasy as supremely valid, and then to make it the sole fantasy anyone can ever think. They make up the most ambitious alliance of playground bullies, and they are the most devastating units of midwittery: they are halfwits with a spellbook, looking up an enchantment they are bound to misread, and throwing people in cauldrons to make sure their magic sticks.

The Counter-Culture that Isn't

I hear the expression *the culture-war*, and it makes me cringe. For one, I see no culture in this alleged war: just a financial status-quo designed to oppress, and the promise of a revolution designed to oppress us further; I see a side that teaches us that school is pointless and that teachers do not deserve good pay, and a side that tries really hard to make school pointless and teachers deserving of no pay; a side that thinks we make excellent cannon-fodder, and a side that thinks women and minorities make just as good cannon-fodder – none of this is metaphorical.

The term suggests the presence of at least two different cultures, one set against the other, all kinds of smaller movements and subcultures joining their ranks or turning coats, one winning at one instance, another the next, the winner the mainstream trend, the other a counter-culture. Of these, it is always the latter that is deemed the nobler competitor – the one that tries to appeal to the young and make itself the righteous ruler, though at present an undeserving victim and therefore the just rebel. This sympathy for the loser is to be expected, seeing as it is innocents that suffer the most in war; it is they who struggle to stay alive, and to rebuild what would never have been destroyed had it not been for the aggressive mandate of their rulers.

The irony in that is that the struggle for dominance has become, on account of the appeal of rebellion, a struggle for rebellion, i.e. a struggle to become a permanent counter-culture: to oppose the man and to stand for the people! though also a struggle, being a project of the privileged, to remain privileged and to have the backing of the many and to be crowned their king. And so, what we see are two elite camps, making themselves out to have been treated unjustly, claiming to stand with the little man, all the while fighting tooth and claw to distance themselves from such filth as the little man. We see millionaires telling you how much they have suffered because they got bad press. The rich and famous person who got canceled is to be pitied because he is being oppressed in spite of being the king. Us plebeians, however, we must not complain of our own misfortunes, because it is noble blood alone that must never be shed. Come what may, we are designated to suffer, for our only alternative is to suffer more. We must be oppressed lest we get oppressed! This is Economy 101. Keep in mind, the king joins us in our oppression – he suffers as much as we do when they tax him as they tax us. Therefore, praise him and pity him and do not forget to worship him, for he is a ruler a martyr and a rebel, and you his subject all the more fortunate to ever remain so.

*

If I seem overly critical of the conservative right, it is not for being a sympathizer of the progressive left. The reason I make fun of the former to a greater degree is because I do not think the latter need me to do it for them – in terms of making a joke of themselves, the progressive left have proven exceptionally independent.

I do not say this as a centrist either. I am not a so-called fence-sitter. On the contrary, it is *because* I have beliefs that I reject the two camps, which, standing for nothing, can only appeal to people who prefer *nothing* to an actual commitment. If you think in terms of left and right, or even of liberals and conservatives, you are really thinking of nothing whatsoever – it is only an ornamental hue you have chosen – a cultural skin; ideologically, *you* are the neutral party. The unaffiliated are the only ones who have taken a side. The only people who will not compromise, who will not sell out, and who actually stand for something.

It annoys me that the terms *left* and *right* even exist. On their own, they tell us nothing about a given movement. A direction is not a destination, let alone our means of getting there. Political camps worldwide, associated with the generalization we today recognize as left and right, to which all camps claim some degree of fealty, are unable to explain their values without additional epithets.

The so-called left wing tends to call itself the progressive left. The problem with that is that progress simply refers to a forward motion: in connotation vaguely positive, but, at the core of its sense, deprived of context as it is, as long as you keep putting road behind you, you are progressing... somewhere. I am yet to learn where. It seems as though they have only muddled left and right by adding yet another dimension as opposed to an explanation. I hear the expression *individual liberties* spoken by some of its representatives, as in they progress towards the furthering of individual liberties. I suppose it makes sense, seeing as the movement is also known as the liberal left, but in that case, its adherents ought to live, work, and theorize according to this concept: it is their job to secure the individual liberties of all law-abiding citizens; they are to be held accountable for any loss of individual liberties under their rule, as well as for any law that, parading as a personal liberty, has instead proven to be but the freedom to err, i.e. it has led people to harm. Failing to meet any of those criteria, it would be a movement of favoritism, selective tyranny, or arbitrary anarchy. Ironically, that is exactly what the progressive left appears to be worldwide. Therefore, I will have none of it.

The conservative right fail to realize that they are just as conceptually empty. They are yet to define whatever it is they are trying to conserve. It cannot be traditional values (nor any virtues, I should add) that they look to conserve, seeing as their moral absolute depends on the voting demographics to which they aim to appeal. One can talk about the virtues of selling out if he so desires, but to talk about being a sellout while remaining virtuous is nonsense. It is even worse that, not letting go of their claim to the conservation of virtue, the right wing makes up the movement that is the most likely to betray virtue. At least the liberal leftist is consistent in disliking virtue and business practices alike if they stand in the way of whatever he deems personal liberties. A conservative, by contrast, though he considers himself the moral party, will dismiss morality if an instance of immorality means protecting capitalism. It is their thing: *the free market!* though they cannot answer *free from what* and *free to do what.* If it means a market free from regulation and free to do whatever it wills, then it is not a free market, but a tyrannous market. It is only a dictator that gets to do anything and everything. It is of little benefit to evoke here the nonaggression principle to make tyranny sound mellow: *yes, the rich man does as he wills, but only as long as it does not infringe upon the liberties of others!* they claim, and they believe it. It is all nonsense. Forcing people into slavery is not nonaggression; discouraging workers' movements is not nonaggression either; weapons manufacturers swimming in money are not a sign of a nonaggressive society; keeping the masses docile under threat of poverty is not it either; ensuring that they always remain just one degree above crippling poverty is (you guessed it) the opposite of liberties uninfringed. It is all the more ironic that, still on the moral front, it is this moral party that advocates the extinction of moral people and the propagation of wicked people. I am not talking about billionaires alone, but the career choices of the average person. Between a writer, a schoolteacher, and a pornographer, which do you think will *make it* in modern society? There is no point in guessing – teachers are barely surviving, most writers do not even get to that point, and pornographers are well-off. Bankers too – I only mentioned perverts in my example as they are the likelier to cause disgust, though, between the two, it is the latter that harm society the most. The best professions among men flounder in mud, and the worst among us prosper unimpeded, making the masses worse in the process, for it is in the interest of profit to have an incult, uneducated, unprincipled population. Any movement with capitalism as its unalterable postulate sponsors prostitutes and drug-dealers (and not just the literal illegal kind, mind you). The conservative right-winger might protest: *but of course we can limit profit somewhat! We can make sexual immorality illegal! We can demand that food-manufacturers stop poisoning our food!*

It is allowed under our system – to have some regulation of businesses! It is good of him to point that out: profit is not the end of morality – even in a free-market society; but if we allow that the market should be regulated when it commits immoralities, even at the expense of profit, does it not also follow that affordable healthcare should be a conservative goal? Just how does one argue morally that people should perish from treatable diseases just because they cannot afford to pay for the treatment – that it is tolerable that businessmen should be incentivized, moreover, to charge insane amounts of money for said treatments? On that note, why are students punished for wanting to study with enormous debt? Why do we penalize intellect? Why are young people being discouraged from living like men – like rational beings endowed with curiosity and intelligence, and are instead nudged towards long hours in manual labor? Their intellectual faculties irrelevant for business, they must ever aspire to serve as non-rational meat-agents. Dignity is a human right. If your political movement discourages dignity in the name of profit, it is not a moral political movement. The only thing you are conserving are the riches of the richest.

While libertarians might not care for morality, I should here add that they are the least intellectually endowed among the right-wingers. They have liberty in their root, and yet they speak in favor of a tyrannous market. Their stance, they have based on a shameful ignorance of history, and poor interpretations of the present state of affairs. They warn against big governments, not realizing that any cabal of rich people is an international government – one we do not elect, and one we cannot vote out of office: not restrained by law or officials they cannot bribe or a moral code they must not break, accountable to nobody but themselves. And for all of their fearmongering about communism (as if criticism of capitalism can only ever be Stalinism), they fail to understand that, whereas there is zero risk of Mao Zedong knocking down my front door to take everything I own, and only a minor risk of his reincarnation, there is presently the very real risk of the private sector taking everything I own if I cannot pay my bills on time. With natural resources and public services usurped by the powerful rich as if conquered by foreign armies, with rising prices and diminishing paychecks, I would not be surprised if we are indeed witnessing the end of private property; but it is not Ho Chi Minh that brings it about, but the inbred child of Johnny Freedom: Peter Laissez-Faire. They employ despicable rhetoric to make their case: they try to portray the abolitionist as a man who envies the slave-owner for having white skin, and they occasionally remind us of our hypocrisy that, though we complain of the air being polluted, we nonetheless refuse to live at the bottom of the ocean. That a lot of flooded cities were the doing of western imperialism, is knowledge that eludes their sensibilities. Backed into the dystopian corner, they tend to argue that this is not real capitalism, but a perverted version of it: crony capitalism, they call it, which, they argue, on account of its reliance on the government, is in reality a kind of socialism. Again, the libertarian fails to realize (besides the meaning of socialism of course) that every capitalist society eventually becomes a crony capitalist society. From what we know, socialism, as the libertarian defines it, is really just the final form of capitalism. By libertarian reasoning, we had best put an end to capitalism before it ushers in the much-dreaded socialism, as it invariably does. But I suppose human nature applies only to the masses and the governments they elect; the powerful rich are incorruptible. This is supposed to be the party of reason, of cold, hard reality, and of liberty. The way I see it, it is only a slaver's fable, concluding in the erasure of human sensibilities. No, I will have none of the right either.

You can see then, Dear Reader, why to stand for something in this life means to stand for no major political movement in the present reality. Political movements, empty in meaning as they are, might as well stand for the literal axes of their designations: they move either left or right, signifying nothing but brute direction, and what is either progress into arbitrarily selective tyranny, or the conservation of a financially selective tyranny. Whatever other questions might cause the two sides to clash, have little bearing on what is really happening. It is not freedom to know the gender of your property; nor is it rebellion to question the gender of state property. The powerful getting even more powerful does not make the poor richer – nor does making the poor pathetic ameliorate their poverty.

*

Now that I have said enough to earn the dislike of both sides, I will conclude this chapter with the observation over which I chose its title, or why we do not have a significant counter-culture in the present day: there is an ideological overlordship presiding over every intellectual decision – everything must conform to one of two dominant trends, which, being trends, are of the dominant culture and admit no such thing as a *counter-* prefix. Neither is the voice of the oppressed; each promotes but one oppression as the antidote to another; they both believe in necessary evils and consider goodness a privilege; they see the youngest of mankind as property (one of the state, one of the parents); and love is something that should be either economized or perverted, which is the worst of all their fallacies.

They have not a clue as to what the most important words mean. It is how I know they are each a facet of the same culture: it is the culture of anti-enlightenment, distaste for language, the anti-intellectual movement, the mechanization of mankind, our regressive plight into hordes. Not only does neither constitute a *counter-*culture, but neither of the two sides is really *culture* at all.

*

There is an illiteracy-machine hard at work. It is meant to turn the majority of mankind into the modern vernacular variety of peasant, namely the barely functional, uneducated idiot who knows but mindless toil and base pleasure; the drunk, dirty, debaucherous halfwit next to whom a midwitted monarch appears divine.

137

It is the blight of our age, I have pointed out already, and the true flaw of modern education, that princes are taught the philosophy of peasants and peasants are taught the arrogance of princes. It does us little good to say that the medieval peasant was not at all like that. Keep in mind, when princes were taught to think like peasants, it was not to the detriment of the princes – it was rather to devalue the peasants, for, since the two classes have existed, peasants have been taught to think like princes; a peasant who thought like a peasant could not have lasted long.

No, the illiteracy machine is not a naturalizing machine meant to turn us into what we really are, but into what we are not. Traditionally, it has been the bards who, creating works so in-tune with nature, maintained the barrier between true identity and unnatural perversion. But how can the bards do what they ought to when, working with language and trading in pleasure of a non-base variety, they encounter patrons-to-be who have never cared to learn about either? I suppose the only thing left to do is to call out the machine and hope that not all prospective patrons have yet seeded their land with plastic.

<u>The Illiteracy Machine</u>

What better proof of illiteracy than the consistent misunderstanding of literature? I have in mind the kind of literature with which kids first practice reading: fairy tales. Failure to understand fairy tales, I hope we can all agree, can be considered, without risk of snobbery, evidence of illiteracy. Now, do not get me wrong: fairy tales are not stories for illiterate or barely literate people – though they might have begun as such in their oral tradition, they are actually among the better literature one can choose to read, seeing as they are on the level of most flash fiction, but significantly richer culturally. They are at once sublime and simple, creative and down to earth, and meant to entertain and teach at the same time; they more often than not succeed. Tolkien had a lot of respect for the genre, calling collections of fairy tales "attics and lumber-rooms," among which "may occasionally be found a thing of permanent virtue: an old work of art, not too much damaged, that only stupidity would ever have stuffed away," which is as perfectly worded a description, more sincere than it is flattering, as can be expected of the pioneer of modern fantasy, which is really the epic descendant of the fairy tale.

We have all heard that classic format, of a wizard granting a good man a blessing on the condition that he uses it for good, a bad man stealing the blessing intending to use it for his own gain alone, but, upon failing the wizard's condition, the villain is outed for what he is. I have encountered people who would hear such a story and say of the villain that his plight was the result of tactlessness: had he allowed the poor man on the boat, had she shown compassion to the talking mouse, had they dealt differently with their brother, our antagonists would have won. I have no doubt, many consider such an outcome the best of all worlds: the villain had such a good time doing whatever they wanted, they expended so little effort in getting everything they wanted, and, with a little tact, they could have enjoyed having it all forever after. If only they were just a bit smarter!

People who think this way tend to live according to the same moral: they are unashamedly villainous, proudly compassionless, and lazy in as many circumstances as they are permitted; but as soon as they have encountered a person fit for a wizard or a prince in the shape of a bear or such an archetype thereby, they adapt an honorable, well-bred, and modest demeanor. Sucking up to authority, they hope to gain the wizard's blessing but shirk his condition. What they fail to recognize is that these stories do not emphasize how the villain tripped up, but the fact *that* he tripped up – the specifics of his downfall are irrelevant; his wickedness became visible not because he failed to hide it, but because it was wickedness. There can be no happy ending if evil has its way. The villains in these tales fail the moral condition as soon as the story begins – it is their *tragic flaw*, if you will: it is their fate to perish.

Insensitivity to the proper moral of a story leads to all kinds of misinterpretations, in culture and outside it. People do not understand the concept of a happy ending. They do not really want one – a happy ending – they only want their *preferable* ending. Happy is irrelevant, for they can be happy without it. Businessmen in bards' skins are quick to comply with this demand: they make TV series and comics and video games and movies and books where the protagonist is a brutal killer, an arrogant billionaire, a suave douchebag, but always, in the end, a person with an agreeable resolution: he wins he gets the girl and he gets to go home safe; he loses nothing except for perhaps a friendly side-character.

This is not how things are in reality. People who have killed in war do not come out unscathed. The same goes for people who kill others treasure-hunting. You do not get to return to your family, having orphaned so many other families, and live a happy suburban life. Nor do you get to become a decent person while enjoying the pleasures that made you insufferable. It is not a deep story either, keep in mind, that, while showing a character who suffers, makes this suffering so attractive in appearance, so heroically emotional or so ruggedly tough, that people would be willing to undergo it. Tragedy is not an ornament. Ornament is not nature. For it is nature alone that can give us the *good* ending, the real ending, the one to which its nymphs and elves and wise old men and women testified through their prophecies and their warnings and their tests of character. The restoration of all good things is the only good ending. The preference for the mere alteration of things to appear just right is but a deception resulting from a deficiency in whichever faculties make up one's receptivity to wisdom. Because appearances can be deceiving. Is that not a common moral in fairy tales? Then again, to people concerned with making up stories rather than telling good stories, i.e. those who put fancy before imagination, anything goes. An illiterate crowd would have it no other way.

*

The inspiration for this chapter began with my observation of what is regarded as nerd-culture. The term refers to media for people who like fantasy and science-fiction, who read books about wizards and spaceships or as of recent wizards on spaceships, who collect comic books and make indie games and watch TV series about girls with swords. I was originally going to give the phenomenon its own chapter. I was going to call it *Nerd Culture was a Mistake.*

There used to be a time when the romantic nerd was somewhat comparable to a nonconforming outcast. While not discriminated against to the same degree, they did things that were not considered cool – theirs was an underground culture, and they had knowledge that was in many ways secret knowledge; they knew about mythology and obscure writers and they dreamed of epic things. It took certain qualification, or an intellectual requirement, to be considered a nerd. But now, nerds are just a trendy congregation of hipsters. It is another counter-culture that isn't. If at all interested in literature, they only care about milk-toast popular writers, commercialized to no end; enormous businesses cater to them; they have elitist circles with group hierarchies; they socialize at costume-parties, they waste money on flashy merchandise, they get wasted and smoke weed and sleep around. I remember the first time I witnessed triangular nerd-drama in person: it was the voluptuous girl dressed as a comic-book character with a whip getting into an argument with the girl dressed as a 16-bit character with a big head over a gangly chinless guy dressed as a comic-book character with a plastic assault rifle. This was during a public event.

The kind of manchild that is now considered a nerd was originally called a dork, a subclass that seems to have appropriated nerdhood due to their newfound sociability. This new breed has jettisoned the values that made up the intelligent nerd, and has instead glorified the ornament with which he used to be associated.

Outside of fashion, they do not stand apart from the uninitiated majority in any significant way. It used to be that a nerd, well-read and conditioned to desire something better than what he saw in the common man, looked upon the hedonism of the simple masses, shook his head, and though, *Brave new world.* Now is a time when that same nerd, having read only a little, and desiring nothing of any particular value, looks upon the hedonistic masses and thinks to himself: *Hell yeah! Brave new world!* This is in spite of the fiction they consume; in spite of stories about humanity rising above its base desires; stories about enchanted forests with creatures of pure intent; about epic quests against evil, about the endless pursuit of knowledge; courage and self-sacrifice in the name of the good. There was a time when people were literate enough to understand Tolkien. Now, they cannot even understand fairy tales. Ours is an era in which orcs are the cool warrior race, elves are hot, and dwarves are alcoholics with anger-management issues. But at least they are not effeminate like elves – and you can quote me on that.

*

Illiteracy leads to universal misunderstanding – to the butchering of all of language, including essential language. We regard the concept of friendship and we misread it as a fable; we then look at our friends and mark them as persons of interest; if they do not do the same, we mark them as *fools.* We miswrite our own names as a collection of achievements, and we misread our individual identities as the things we present for others to see. It is among the scariest of misreadings when a doctor looks at you and he does not read *patient* but *customer.* It is second only to a politician misreading *citizen* as *subject.* There is illiteracy all over. Even easy three-letter words like *car* are being misread as a lot of things they are not. The definition of love has been made the task of midwits, and pleasure has been demoted to the opium of the peasants. Dear Reader, words are too important a thing to be left to an illiterate generation.

We are turning feral in spite of our technology, and we become unnatural as a result of our regression. It is in our nature to progress, not to become one with the wilderness whence we came. It is an illusion, a fallacy that in nobler times would have been considered lunacy: the idea that the rational animal becoming rational is a deviation from nature; that civilization was a mistake; that the only good mind is an absent one. The global mental health crisis (as we like to call it) is really just an unparalleled point of stupidity: of illiteracy and orphanage (take that as symbolically as you will), beginning with a spike in loneliness: with people being convinced that other people are irrelevant, then, as the conviction took hold, that they are themselves irrelevant; culture making indifference into a virtue, and businesses making a pleasant experience of alienation.

Girard's Gallows

The lowest point of the prevailing tendency that is at once stupefaction and alienation is the ongoing genocide of which only a few are aware and regarding which even less care sincerely. It is the dehumanization of a group of people, who, through no fault of their own, have been mistreated and abused and ignored and are only addressed with but two arguments: the gaslighting that they do not get to consider themselves mistreated, balanced with the deflection that, if they are indeed mistreated, they are wrong to think it anyone's fault but their own. When somebody addresses them with a show of respect or seeming concern for their mistreatment, it is but faked respect and a self-righteous, virtue-signaling concern.

It is cruel beyond reason, the degree of discrimination they face, having committed no crime deserving of the judgment; this is to the extent that any conversation about them must begin with the speaker, if he intends to defend them, explicitly stating that he is not one of them. He is but a noble stranger, he says, doing a service to these subhuman fiends, whom he would not call fiends directly for he is their noble protector, though he might as well do it, seeing as he only reinforces the discrimination against them by so fervently distancing himself from them. *You may trust me*, his reasoning goes, *for I am not like these brutes!* As if a lawyer defending a murderer must first make it explicitly clear that he himself is not also a murderer, or discussing celebrity rape allegations, one must first state that he is not a rapist. This minority is so loathed, that the moment they come up in conversation, any suspicion that one is of them must be eliminated before any discussion can take place, a disclaimer seldom employed even when debating the most heinous crimes. They are vilified because they are ostracized, and they are ostracized because of their alleged villainy. If you have spent any time on the internet, you know I am talking about incels.

When I first heard the term, and I learned that it stands for *involuntary celibate*, I thought that it refers to just about every man at some point in his life. I did not expect to hear, right after, that an incel is not just any man down on his luck, but specifically the most disgusting kind of man – comprising a tiny minority of misfits, an incel, I was told, was a terrorist: a sexless man so deprived of the pleasure that he goes on to commit violent crime. It sounded absurd. It was as if a bad science-fiction writer had just learned about Freud. It was in the same string of speech, spoken by a conservative man, that incels were described to me as left-wingers, who, frustrated that there is no big government to give them girlfriends, lash out against western society and its values. This information-dump led me to believe, for a while, that the phenomenon must be a myth – that whatever violent crimes have been recorded, their tracing back to some far-left group called incels is like blaming the slaughter of goats on the chupacabra.

You can imagine my bewilderment the next time I encountered the expression, having in the meantime forgotten about it, when it was explained to me as a movement of conservative right-wingers, who, scared of losing their white privilege, lash out against women and minorities, whose prosperity they envy. Furthering my exposure to the internet, I also read that they are an inert group of losers, not capable of doing anything, sitting around in their basements, and hating modern entertainment for having female characters. The person who said this observed that they hate seeing women in media because they are too scared to approach women in real life. They have no experience interacting with the opposite sex whatsoever, this *intellectual* explained, in a serious but mocking tone, and, if I read him well, a tinge of gloating, spite, and not a small degree of pride at being in the position to say it. When I told an acquaintance, in a different conversation altogether, that some women take pleasure in manipulating men, this person accused me of being an incel – he let me know that incels pursue women and feel manipulated as they are led on and ultimately rejected.

The cumulative definition I was to derive then, I suppose now congruent with the illiteracy machine, was that an incel is a creature that is at once an extreme leftist and an extreme right-winger, who wants a woman so badly he hates all women, and has therefore turned a violent criminal who does nothing but complain about video games and TV series, because of which he never talks to women, who continually reject him as he keeps pursuing them from his basement that he never leaves.

*

But there is something else to observe here, which *is* in line with the confused descriptions I have presented above: incel is the new Nazi. As Godwin's Law has proven the staple of lowbrow rhetoricians, there developed the need for another derogatory group in which to lob one's opposition: an ad-hominem that, not as easy to disprove as political affiliation, would also be such a horrible thing, such a loathed concept in society, that the efforts of one's opponent will instantly shift to defending himself that he is certainly not *it* – better yet, a word which employment would grant instant victory to the one who has employed it, for, being such an effective toxin, it poisons the well, the soil, and all the local gentry with its mere evocation. Given the motive, it makes sense that right-wingers call incels socialists and left-wingers call them right-wingers. It is identical to the treatment of Nazis in political discourse. Each side claims it is the other that is to blame for the rise of supreme evil.

Now, a midwitted person might be reading this, smirking at my observation regarding the confused definition. *Well it could be that some incels are right-wing and some of them are left-wing, and that some of them talk to women and others don't – there is no contradiction,* he thinks, as is expected of a midwit, never realizing that, if the case is such, then incels are too general a demographic to treat as one collective; to project any individual behavior as representative of the whole is as if to blame all of Germany for enabling Godwin's law. In short: incels are neither left-wing nor right-wing nor violent nor misogynistic nor aggressive nor inert – they are simply people suffering from extreme loneliness. The definition of incelhood then, ought to be as it was in its original conception, i.e. whatever unites all these different people with different personalities and different beliefs into the same collective referent: involuntary celibacy – a status, please note, applicable to just about every man at some point in his life.

Its universal applicability explains why so many have been so quick to accept it as an insult: it is simple projection. Just look at all the lonely people who would convince you that they are not incels – they just *haven't found the right one yet!* or they are too busy with work, or they need to take care of some personal issues before they go looking for a woman – *but incels,* they assure you, they are *certainly not!* They do not seem to realize that their personal issues or work or inability to find *the right one* are not voluntary decisions: if they are lonely now, they are lonely involuntarily. It is the same with the MGTOW movement, who claim they do not pursue romance because there are no quality women left. One wonders if there being no quality women is a state of affairs the MGTOW movement chose voluntarily. It is the modern bachelor's best-kept secret: knowing that they have been involuntarily celibate, or, alternatively, knowing that they could turn involuntarily celibate at any moment, they hope to guard against this by twisting the expression into some horrid creature of the kind they could never be – a smelly obese criminal or an embittered loser of the enemy's political camp. Having adopted it as a hyperbolic insult, they feel safe against the accusation that condemns men – and women – to such segregated fates, even if a fluke of fortune does happen to nudge them that way: at least they are not *that* bad.

The *Merriam-Webster* dictionary defines the word like so: "a person (usually a man) who regards himself or herself as being involuntarily celibate and typically expresses extreme resentment and hostility toward those who are sexually active." What I say next is not criticism of the dictionary itself, as it only presents the word as it is most commonly used, in which case it is the correct definition. With that said, semantically speaking, it is the wrong definition. It is as if to say that *holly* typically means *sacred* because people commonly misspell *holy*. The two examples of the word in context are from texts meant to present incels as the most repulsive of villains; one of them reads: "'In recent years, a number of these men [mass murderers] have identified as so-called incels... men who express rage at women for denying them sex and who frequently fantasize about violence and celebrate mass shooters...'" (Arango et al.). That is harsh. Even worse, it is incorrect. We do not define a gamer as *a person who frequently fantasizes about violence and celebrates war criminals*, though that is his hobby. We do not contextualize *a jock* as somebody who *numbs his brain and typically expresses extreme tribalism regarding sports* – at least not in any official dictionaries. I do not suppose any part of the entry for *rapper* includes the kinds of fantasies the typical rapper tends to promote in his music. Why should the entry for incels be any different? There is no reason to assign specific cultural connotation to a general demographic in a medium that primarily deals with denotative sense. It is wrong to assume hostility in any case. But perhaps that is the goal: people are meant to feel disdain for the incel; to imagine him as the villain, the person with whom they can never commiserate – the eternal stranger. It is a convenient ornament – a scapegoat by which to ignore the real problem of alienation, and attribute so much vileness to a marginalized group instead of all the other factors we would rather not consider.

The most offensive instance of midwittery when addressing incels, however, is committed by people who think they are doing good – the moralistic group that tries to explain things by some rational means that they know best, these rational means being the mainstream narrative reiterated. Not concerned with what incels actually believe, and having read only second-hand accounts of this creature they so compassionately loathe, they tend to argue like so: *incels are lonely people, who, instead of looking inward, into their own character flaws as the reason for their loneliness, they project their shortcomings onto women.* I hereby pronounce anybody who has ever said this or believed it or worse yet made educational content with it, and fails to repent of it to this day, the worst variety of midwit, with all their other past and future intellectual work, generally of mediocre quality anyway, being totally nullified on account of this error against the most marginalized among us. Even a precursory glance at what incels say reveals how stupid it is to propose that it must be projection in which incels engage the most. For one, incels are not at all opposed to the idea of self-improvement. They have such expressions as *gymcel* and *selfcel*, which refer to incels who try to make themselves better by working out at the gym, and incels who read self-help books with the same goal in mind. The flaws over which they feel rejected are flaws that, not projected onto the opposite sex, they consider to be their own inborn shortcomings; you should be able to tell their position by such self-derogatory coinages as *baldcel viocecel shortcel minoritycel poorcel autistcel dumbcel* or *cripplecel.* That last one should tell you that crippled people are also part of this group society so readily demonizes. Incels are in reality an unfortunate community that have been dealt a bad hand in life – not some entitled, violent monster for pseudointellectuals to denigrate.

*

Now, it is true that some incels harbor a lot of rage. But it is to no greater degree than the violent tendencies exhibited by non-incels. It makes little sense to villainize one group for universals we seldom care to point out in others. Bullying in schools is not done by incels (though it is likely to create incels), crime on the streets is not committed by people without partners, and crime in high places is certainly not the product of a sexless demographic. Now, I am not trying to downplay acts of violence associated with incels – I condemn any and every such act: assault is not morally justified, and it accomplishes nothing. With that said, incels do not have it in their aspirations to commit crime; the only thing they want is a partner, and the only thing they want in lieu of a partner is what they call *cope* – if they are sentenced to live alone, they only ask that you leave them alone; occasionally they vent (feel free, Dear Moralist, to cast the first stone) and, in the communities they form, they make their philosophies on why the world is as it is: they form a *counter-culture that is*, whether you agree with it or not.

With that in mind, seeing as there is nothing inherently violent in incel ambitions, the thing to ask is whether the violence associated with individual incels originates within the individual himself, or if it is an external influence. In the case of the former, it has very little to do with the state of incelhood, but is rather just another manifestation of the mental health crisis in the western world (to be analyzed on a per-case basis, not regarded as inherent to the demographic); if it comes from outside, however, that would suggest that it is society that creates deviance where there should be none. It is not an unlikely explanation. Is it not ironic that, on the one hand, people believe it is isolation that causes incels to go rogue, but their primary response to this is to isolate them further? Or that, despite believing that incels are sex-crazy, just about every mainstream trend promotes sex-craze? That we criticize them for their self-centeredness in a self-centered world, or that, accusing them of being violent and impressionable, we keep impressing upon them that they are violent?

Of the fallacies adopted by the demographic, all I see is but the logical conclusion to the fallacies we are all fed. They believe in alpha males and beta males. They believe that men and women only exist to mate and that mating is the only thing that matters – all else is cope. They believe that women are attracted to testosterone, and that men who show little or no signs of it are bound to perish. Theirs is a Darwinistic worldview. You are either fit to mate, or you are not fit to survive. These are all wrong. Some I have addressed already; the others are just as silly. If brute testosterone were attractive, men would not be shaving their necks backs and loins, and a bald pate would be considered beautiful. Regarding genes, the jury is still out on why looking cute in glasses trivializes a genetic flaw such as myopia, or why, if good genes are the determiner of sexual attraction, a woman is not instantly repulsed by a man who, handsome though he is, has a sibling with an inborn disability. But as poorly thought out as they are, these theories do not differ much from what the average person believes. The only differences between incel philosophy and the philosophy of the average person is that, not having as many pleasurable distractions, compared to the average person, the incel has had more opportunities to think, and so he has taken the dominant worldview to its logical conclusion. It is not a perversion of modernity, what he believes, but modernity in its true form.

Incels are not a problem, but a reflection of the problem. They show all that is wrong with society: the alienating tendency of modern living, commercialized aesthetics, distrust and disloyalty, corporate morals, rampant opportunism, elitist mentality taught as a virtue... the incel reflects all of these issues right back at us. Deprived of the natural, psychological, and spiritual right to a mate, destined to suffer for a wrong he never committed, the equivalent of the sick and the poor in Biblical times, marginalized as he is by the fortunate majority (including the Biblical majority), all because those of us who *got lucky*, to varying extent, are willing to uphold a tyrannous system as long as it keeps us in its favor (to varying extent). It is no wonder – the tendency to either villainize them as superbly disgusting or else ignore them altogether: men need it to soothe their conscious.

Neglecting to acknowledge any of this, there are analysts who accuse the incel of an innately toxic character (whatever that means) that women sense in him no matter how nice he tries to be, which is the reason they – justifiably – find him repulsive. That is just stupid. Exactly what reason do we have to assume that these women must have a sixth sense for judging character, such that, incels, twisted as they are, cannot deceive with kindness what telepathy reveals for wickedness? Are we really prepared to also allow the implication that, given the clairvoyant attribute we have made up, women who are victims of abusive partners got into these abusive relationships knowingly? We cannot go on dabbling in fancy if our ambition is to actually address the problem. Then again, that *is* part of the problem: the fact that we do not really care to address it in the first place – explaining it away is ever the preferable course of action. People are ready to evoke magic as long as it means they get to ignore the inconvenience that is accountability. They are so eager to villainize, moreover, that they are ready to throw yet another demographic to the wolves in the process, and all for the license to call the smell of decay a novel perfume.

There has been a tear in how we see the world. Cognitively, we do not look through our own eyes, as have our ancestors before us, but through the whims of trend. Even to the extent that many are fine with body dismorphic disorder being encouraged among the young, along with the actions they take related to the disease, some self-destructive, others merely stupid: of such a dumb thing as mewing to get a big jawline, seeing as we have never evolved past the equine standard; of male hairloss being treated as leprosy, now that we see hair-clinics advertised at every other billboard; of short men being erased from the record of men, now that it is the one institutionally legal racism; of people with otherwise functional teeth wearing braces well into their twenties – then of girls, still in their twenties, having taken off their braces, considering plastic surgery for their wrinkles; of filters on phones meant to turn natural skin into porcelain, now that the makeup industry stands to gain divinity; of unnaturally muscular actors, now that *supplements* have been normalized in fitness. We see psychologists ignore and on occasion promote this as normalcy instead of fighting it at every step – and I do mean at *every* step, not just the office: virtue on the clock is an oxymoron. In the meantime, people who react to it are judged as unstable. Those who react to it the most, for they also feel it the most, are judged as villains: toxic and evil and disinterested in self-improvement – isolated because sick, sick because of their isolation, and deserving to only grow sicker. This isn't even where the irony peaks regarding the incel-discussion by the way. Just for flavor, think of a middle-aged psychoanalyst with hair plugs calling incels delusional for their obsessions, and you will begin to see just how crazy this subject has really become.

*

What I derive from it all, is that incels have become a social experiment to the effect of permissible extermination – of segregation and eventual annihilation. They are a group – an ever-growing group – that we have collectively decided must be our collective punching bag for as long as they exist. They are an entity unto which we pour all our frustrations, all of our insecurities, and all of our sadistic impulses, be it of the aggressive or the apathetic variety. And as we alternate between turning a blind eye and flashing a gloating stare at the suffering of a demographic, we call upon a primordial urge of mankind in our least flattering state, once thought annulled, now being revived en masse. It is the urge for violence as altered by the instinct for cowardice, namely the longing to inflict the former without fear of retribution – physical, legal, or moral. This makes up the institution of sacrifice.

You could perhaps tell by the title where my argument was headed all along. It is a reference to René Girard, part of whose intellectual legacy emphasizes the role of violence as a motif in civilization, specifically, its development. He imagined ritualistic sacrifice as a means to direct the urge for violence onto an act safe from violent consequence. When this barbaric institution was practiced on living humans, the trick was to first dehumanize the person atop the altar – to make sure that he was an outcast or a criminal or a slave; rarely, a king, but all the same, it was imperative that the man they slaughtered was not *one of their own.*

In the modern day, this role has been assigned to the incel.[32] It is a sacrifice meant to appease many perverse urges – from violence to projection to all kinds of immoral ambitions – and a sacrifice for which we nonetheless cheer, because it gives us the security that we are on the winning team. The incel, as the outcast and the villain that he is, at once born into his own villainy (because of which he is hopeless) and also entirely responsible for it (which makes him unpitiable), is not one of us; he is so unlike us, we remind ourselves, that he is a creature none of us can ever truly become – too pathetic, and too politically disagreeable, you see. We then go on to treat him with the rage that, we believe, is only natural and therefore good and right and a privilege allotted to the best of us – by gods that favor us, and by genes that made us the superior specimens that get to live.

In our treatment of victims so marginalized, we march on, as wordless zombies, into a primitive structure we had thought abandoned for thousands of years, as western civilization, the ornament of the law notwithstanding, begins to give way to its new shape: a cult of the self, alternating with fleeting outbursts of tribalism, making up a global yet disjointed, animalistic yet unnatural, primitive and, ironically, exclusively modern iteration of a horde.

---

[32] Alongside any other group that is proclaimed guilty without cause; it is an open market, the bullying institution, until it eventually becomes a free-for-all as civilization expires completely.

Flash and Fiction

<u>Boy vs Machine</u>

Neither is good. Between the two, the machine, which we recognize is evil, will always win, but its victory is secured on account of the boy being what he is. Without progress, we fail in our purpose, our purpose being to progress. One does not look at a grown man with a childish mind, thinking him the antithesis of the French expression for being late. It is the same with culture. We must mature. The alternative is to perish – some literally, as thoroughly immature people do if left to their own devices, and others in spirit only, arguably worse off, living on as the many inhumanities they have come to emulate, by the process by which feral children adopt the behaviors of beasts.

I am afraid this warning is in the future tense but for a minority of the population – as far as I have seen, for most people, warnings are at this point obsolete. We have already devolved into hordes, en masse, to a bastardized rebirth of civilization, to disloyalty and selfishness and contempt of intellect. We have accepted machines as our superiors, and we have made terrible strides towards assimilation. This decline, I have traced back to the orphaning of pleasure, which is the major hurdle in its reversal: without a proper guide, without the proven record of culture, and without the effort on our part for its attainment, the misunderstanding that undermines cognition and human interaction alike is not a looming threat so much as a matter of course.

I do not blame the average person for this – at least not for most of it. There are many things (major stresses and trivialities alike) that prevent people from becoming as well-read as we wish we were. I have been saying it for years: the easiest way to turn a man into an effective illiterate is to give him a bad chair. Once you have made a person chronically uncomfortable, any effort he might invest into whatever text he has been given to read, be it philosophical, scientific, or an ordinary opinion-piece, will prove secondary to his efforts to balance the pain in the neck, back, and coccyx – indeed, a half-hour read will require hours to finish, provided he does not abandon it in the first twenty minutes. Whatever articles he may have intended to read on his computer will soon become articles he has not read on his computer. If you want to prove him incapable of reading printed content either, put him in a poorly lit room. It is hard to comprehend text one cannot see. Noise pollution is another means to increase the effectiveness of the illiteracy machine. Once you have added the ruckus of vehicles and chatter and television, not only will you have made reading require twice the attention, but the reader will have only half the attention to spare. Next, ensure that a man has no reason to read, make his work dull and his means of entertainment dulling, and you will find a man who reads very little – if at all.

With that in mind, having observed the plight of the reading habits of many, some guilty of it and some only innocently involved in the transgression, I can tell you that most people are not to blame for what is happening – just as people of late antiquity were not to blame for suffering Hunnic raids. Of course, I do not consider any of it a *perfectly* pardonable excuse not to read: we all have an obligation to maintain active intellectual lives; after all, the bravest of the citizenry were apt to join the militia and take up arms against the Hun.

I am aware of some recent attempts to address this, but it seems to me that they all miss the point. I have seen people try to summarize books in a short format – online videos or applications on smart devices intended to tell the story of *War and Peace* in the span of time it takes to drive to the bookstore and purchase *War and Peace*. I have seen abridged literature, and literature of the new kind – with its *gritty writing* and mature themes adapted for modern sensibilities: fast-paced for slow readers, violent and sexual, and all about the storytelling rather than the story. But they all miss the point. For one, tossing the complexity that makes classic literature valuable is not how we return the value of classic literature. We do not help culture by supplanting it with lowbrow entertainment. Never forget that the kind of pleasure that is *really worth it*, in any aspect of life, is the kind of pleasure that a person must labor to acquire. It is a rite of passage. With time, as one improves, its attainment will grow easier, but the first few steps are a feat one must attempt on one's own good will. It is good that editions of Shakespeare have footnotes and ideally lists of potentially unfamiliar words. These help you learn – they make you better at it. But a simplified version of Shakespeare is an artificial version of Shakespeare, i.e. it is *not* Shakespeare. One cannot take away the pleasures of literature hoping to preserve literature; there can be no equivalent in high art to a vitamin supplement in nutrition.

Nor do the political sympathies of people working in culture matter in the slightest. I am not telling artists not to have political opinions – only to realize that it is not political opinions that make books into classics or poems worth reading. The only thing they make them is *well-reviewed*. Politics interfering with art, not as an element observed, but as an argument being made, adds an artificiality to the art being produced, which makes it – you guessed it – *not* art, for it is in reality propaganda. The fact that sponsorship is reserved for activists is to the detriment of art and artist alike. The fact that the kind of art for which one does not need a wealthy sponsor is also a kind of art that cannot really hope to reach very many people is to the detriment of all mankind.

One must wonder why it is the case that the conditions for creating and experiencing art are becoming not easier, but, nearing impossibility, a welcome obsoleteness, and if, seeing as most of us will, at the very least, agree that the world is not as it should be, there might be a correlation between the discouragement of intellect and the worsening of the world. The illiteracy machine is a mighty beast indeed – it can target groups and individuals directly, and it can indirectly radiate stupidity onto unsuspecting subjects.

But I propose that, even though orphaned pleasure is the reason that bards are being ignored, it is not orphaned pleasure where the final battle is lost (and with it the future of mankind). Fortunately, there is one other stronghold that we might yet defend, and, from it, we may go on to reconquer the once-tame lands now-turned barbaric. It is the fact of understanding. If we may understand one another, however few of us remain, we may yet succeed.

Two Fables

Someplace in Sweden, luxuriously rural, in the second most luxurious house in the village, there lived a village chief and his son. In this same village, there was also the palace of a king whose daughter the aforementioned son was to someday marry. Having noticed that they liked each other, and being good friends with the chief, the magnanimous king arranged it: when they come of age, the two will be wed. When he learned of this, the village chief sat down with his son and spoke to the boy like so:

"You grow wise and strong, and when you are old enough, you will inherit all of this – my house, which shall become yours, our horses, one of which you own already, our valuables, which value I hope to make all the greater by the time you get to partake in it; above all else, you will have for your bride a princess of immeasurable beauty, made all the better for her character – for her grace and her graciousness and her loyalty to all the people of the kingdom. Just please, for your sake, stay clear of the border, for it is unsafe, and I could not bear the thought of losing you. After all, you have plenty of things to do in the safety of our homestead."

They were happy for some time, but it was not long before raiders descended upon the village, wherefrom they hailed nobody knows, and carried off with their bounty some villagers who lived close to the border, indefensible as it was, including the son of the village chief, who happened to be playing there, contrary to his father's advice. The chief set out search parties, and so did the king. Their search for the boy, however, proved in vain.

The old man's grief grew as the years went by. Although he might have been relieved to know that the boy was alive, he would not have been as content to hear that, having been made a slave to the raiders, he was at the mercy of people most merciless. The suffering the boy endured in captivity was torture the likes of which the chief would not have inflicted even on a guilty criminal, let alone his own kin.

But the boy grew, in spite of his hardships, strong and capable, and so, one day he challenged one of the raiders to a duel. Now a strong man, younger than the raider, and harboring so much rage, he won easily. It was then that the raider-chief proclaimed him his new right-hand man.

"That old idiot was getting sloppy and cared little to serve me; he was a drunken fool and he got what a drunken fool has coming to him! This slave, however, in him I see potential!"

It was shortly after this that the raiders planned another attack on the village where the boy was born. They attacked, stronger than before, and they made their bloody trail all the way to the king's palace. They burst inside the building, and the boy, now a young man, saw the princess, felt a liking to her, and took her as his booty.

"I will satisfy my cravings with this one," he said, "This one is all mine!"

On his way out, pockets filled with gold and the princess on his shoulder, he noticed an old man bowed before him.

"Who might you be, you weakling?" demanded the boy, for he thought he recognized, albeit only vaguely, that grim visage.

The man was no other than his father, formerly the village chief, now the village elder; and so the old man answered:

"I am your father, and you are my son. It was I that raised you until these savages stole you from me, and I was going to give you everything you see before you – it would have been yours: the village you have just pillaged, all the gold you would have needed (much more than you now carry in your pockets), all the horses in my stable, and the woman you now desire unjustly would have been yours in marriage with the king's blessing."

The boy, looking down at the old man, showed no regret for what he had done, but smirked, spat, and muttered through clenched teeth:

"You call yourself a father? You talk big, but look at all the raider-chief has done for me that you never did – *factually*, might I add: how he has let me have all this gold and this beautiful stallion and to claim this woman as my own! What need have I of you, when I have all that I wanted without your help? I am not your son, but a child of the raiders, and all this is my blessing from them!"

*

Now that you have read the story, I assume you can guess what it is about – and why it is set in Sweden. The boy clearly has some kind of Stockholm syndrome. It is an unflattering problem. It is disgraceful to think of oneself as somebody whose psyche should be at once cowardly, weak, and abused to total breakage. You would also be right to condemn the boy for his lack of wisdom: he would have had all that, plus many other things, and so without having had to endure any torture in the meantime, had it been up to his father. Nevertheless, he not only dislikes his father, but he deems the raider-chief – the architect of his misery – his true guardian. It is stupid, psychological issue or not.

What makes me wonder, however, is why so many people exhibit this same exact attitude towards God. I am not talking about belief. I am talking about the hostility they exhibit to the very idea. They show not only an unwillingness to learn, but passionate hatred for the mere concept – they do not care to know what Scripture says unless it is a version they can mock; they will not listen to a man who speaks of theology unless it is a man they can also mock; they will have nothing to do with religion or its imagery unless it is imagery depicting the enemy, who is the only one they will not mock.

They have probably taken offense with my book for even citing Scripture, and certainly at my calling out the Cosmic Stockholmer.

I repeat, this is not about belief or disbelief, but about kneejerk antagonism to the concept. Why they prefer the enemy and disdain the father, even on the level of myth, is beyond me. It is the height of illiteracy to view the inventor of pleasure as the villain, and the corruptor of pleasure as the good guy – on account of pleasure, mind you, to blur the line between irony and idiocy: to misread a tyrant as a rebel and a revolutionary as a wimp.

That nobody has any interest in learning what the religious fuss is all about must be a problem unanswerable within speculation to a reasonable cause. It makes up for a weird dynamic, wherein people are weirded out by religion, allegedly, because too many people talk about the subject, and also where nobody talks about religion so as not to weird people out with the subject. Theology gets a hostile reception that is unreserved for most other topics – most ancient, regressive myths even. Nobody I know has ever hated learning about Homer, despite his long-winded opus or his patriarchal tendencies, or expressed dislike for Odysseys as a bore or a liking to Antinous as a rebel. Therefore, lacking any good explanation to the contrary: Stockholm it is.

The other side, however, is just as weird.

*

Imagine people who worship letters – a string of letters, to be exact, that holds power over the universe: that controls good spirits, that wards from evil, that heals the wounded, that determines the value of man in this life, and is the only arbiter for whether or not he gets another. You might call such a cult bizarre, but the thing is: that cult is likely the most prominent cult in the west.

The modern Christian is really not a Christian as much as a letter-worshipper. To prove it, I have prepared a dialogue you can attempt in real life and find that it is not in every instance hypothetical. Let us begin by asking this cultist exactly who it is that they worship. They will in likelihood tell you that it is Jesus that they worship. If you ask them if this is the only name upon which a person can call to be saved, many will answer that *yes, that is the only name you can call upon to be saved.* Now, if you asked them if they are aware of the fact that the original pronunciation of that name is not Jesus but Yeshua, they will laugh: *Well of course, but it's not the name itself that matters! It is the person for whom the name stands who gets you to Heaven.* Very well. It is a sound a belief as any. But was this person, you may ask them, just any person with that name, i.e. do you worship Him for His name alone? *No, they will say. Of course not! We worship Him for being God!* That is all good, but let us next ask them what God is, and watch the cult of letter-worship begin to rear its head. Let us say, for the sake of argument, that they answer that God is love. This is biblically accurate.[33] So let us then ask them: if God is love, and if you worship Jesus for being God, i.e. for being Love Incarnate, and it is this that gets you to Heaven, does anyone then who worships Love, and by extension, ultimately worships what you also worship, also enter Heaven, even if it is not the same name by which he recognizes Love? Now is the point at which the letter-worshipper reveals his true colors: *Of course not!* he says, *Because he's got the wrong name!* and so you can see, though he does not believe it is letters that lead a man to salvation, according to him, it is only through the worship of letters that a man may be saved.

This should not be controversial in Christian circles. The salvation of people who lived before the resurrection is not a subject of heated debate. Most Christians believe that many good people of the B.C. era have been saved – I doubt that there are any serious theologians who believe that anybody born before that point was born just to go to hell. But here's the thing: if the resurrection had to happen for the salvation of mankind, then it does not follow that the event took place in order to introduce but a new reason for damnation, namely, the lack of belief in it after the fact.

---

[33] You may look up 1 John 4:7-21 as an example – one of many.

Not meaning to step on anybody's beliefs, I am just trying to point out an inconsistency among modern Christian theologians (amateur and professional alike). They think it impossible to worship without the letters. When they make music or write books, they will not do it without referencing the letters; when they look at a man, they look for his mentioning of the letters to help them decide if the man has any chance at all of being good. This turns the faith into an ornament; a cultural mark that comes before all else, including our ability to ascertain beauty and truth and virtue with the good sense we have been gifted. Instead of a liberating word of good news, they make of Christianity an idolatry – a measuring of reality by its external likeliness to an object they associate with divinity, and an object which, its initial motivation notwithstanding, is just the chance of culture and an arrangement of letters.

*

But imagine a world where neither the Cosmic Stockholmer nor the letter-worshipper are subjects to their respective fallacies. Imagine a world where Christians listen to rock-and-roll and insist on secular education, and where atheists read the New Testament and wish that it were true. Imagine a world where neither side allowed the appeal of ornament, be it of faith taken too far or disbelief esteemed too highly, stand between them and understanding.

I am not selling you a utopia of nice people – I hope you do not misread it that way. I am only proposing a state of affairs where people understand what it is they believe, undeceived by ornament, and act accordingly.

Yes, I know I am being optimistic with this, but I titled the chapter *Two Fables* for a reason.

<u>The Sole Promise</u>

Because I do not write this expecting to win. I write expecting to contribute to the good fight – victory is not an expectation of the hopeful, I have come to realize, as much as a deterrent to the same; the odds for its attainment are too low to rally any troops except the kind that, in their naivety, forget that any truly noble fight is a test of endurance, not of accomplishment. Our only hope can be that we are on the right side; that whatever we do is not in vain. Sometimes, it is the fallen warrior who has fallen into greatness, being the only one to escape subjugation, by which analogy we hope that defeat is not always synonymous with failure.

None of this is to say that defeat is a given. I do not write as a defeatist. I only mean to point out that we ought not to be motivated by the prospect of triumph, for in addition to its diminutive likelihood, it is also the wrong goal. For the war on concept, in regards to mankind, the subject to which it always returns, is a war on character and a war of character – it is a war *for* character: those to be eradicated and the one in which all should assimilate.

It is an ongoing discussion, albeit seldom an overt kind of discussion, given the enemy's tendency to silence dissent, waged in practice, in status, and inference, of the kind of character one ought to be: of what arbitrates our whims, what we consider our whims must mean, and how we consider ourselves capable of this consideration. In such a campaign, it is not majority rule that determines winners from losers, seeing as it is a contest for individual personality, not public score. It is character itself that attests to either a fought-for liberty or to the humiliating consent to submission. It is in prospects like these that I am glad, seeing as an artist cannot be but a patriot, that it has been the motto of my people to never surrender.

*

If you have come this far, I think you know what the solution is. For one, it is to get people to listen to one another – first to get them to talk and then to discuss things and not to assume the other side by necessity beguiled or evil – not without proof. It is to shun such divisive and shallow debates as are trendy in popular discourse, and instead call out whoever it is that wants us to have them – be it an idiot who thinks himself smart talking about the current trend, catered as it is to the appetite of the least intelligent among us, or a conniving man who knows all too well that encouragement of stupidity is the path to suzerainty. It is to see the machine for the problem it is, to let other people know about it, and to return bards to positions from which they may continue doing their jobs. Know your history and know what to do with it. I have been saying these things in all my books – here, I just state them explicitly, and consequently not as elegantly. But there is one other thing I would like to bring to your attention before I conclude the chapter. It is the fact of narrative in non-fiction.

It is challenging to write the conclusion to the third set in a trilogy. Especially as it ought to exceed the other two, though the other two were, I now realize, as sublime as I can go with the format. I suppose I can always summarize the book (as I have done already) and call that a conclusion, but I believe I ought to do both: I will therefore try to be sublime for a third time *and* summarize what I have been discussing so far. It would require some semantic compression, of course, and, to my convenience, it is something I have already done – the compression, that is: it is in the cover.

It is a barren waste, whether a desert on Earth or the surface of Mars I cannot tell, although that the rocks in the background resemble urban buildings is deliberate design. Either way, it is an alienating, desolate reality in which the cover is painted. In the foreground, there fights Charles Darwin the man with a robotic version of himself. Whichever way we evolve is up to us. Above the struggle on the ground, and above all else (and in the center of it all, according to the X axis), there is the Star of Bethlehem.

You may see it however you want; I do not worship letters as ornament, so it is all the same to me: God, Love, Wisdom, Beauty, Nature, Being – anything really, as long as it is pure and good and right and honest and perchance real.

On the left, we see three riders pursuing it. They may be the three wise men, going about it methodically and slowly, as befits wise men. However, they may not reach it in time, possibly because of their mellow pace, for to the right there is a galloping quartet chasing after the same prize. The intuitive guess is that this latter group are the four riders of the apocalypse, but I would not end their poetic implications just there. They could be, perhaps, the beast "slouching toward Bethlehem to be born" (Yeats), or they could be the four ministers of my previous book, on their way to lay claim on truth and beauty and being. The outcome of this picture, be it in the background or the foreground, depends on many factors, and I will let the reader decide what they must be.

The real conclusion, of course, the bit of semantic wealth that concludes what I have written, here as well as throughout the rest of this series, is on the back cover. As you finish the book, and as you turn it around, the important thing to understand is the difference between a good fantasy and a bad one, and, once you have chosen a good fantasy, to learn from it which parts were fantastic, and which of them were merely fictional. That makes all the difference.

Which is my concluding statement to the series: understanding is a product of goodness, and goodness is contingent on understanding. Whenever you spot a deviation in either, it is always a disruption in the willingness to be courageous, tolerant, empathetic, merciful, or sincere. Whenever a person disagrees with that, namely he argues that these are not what constitutes goodness, it is a person who does not care to be truly good. I am yet to meet anyone who is all five but believes them to be bad qualities to have.

If moral intelligence is a quintessential element of intelligence, and if intelligence and sanity are identical in effect, then a genius-level intellect and a good man will always find a way to understand one another, as they are both of the same mind; for the greatest of minds constitute the best of us, and the best of us cannot have but the greatest of minds.

In good faith,
Hank Youngman.

END of PART III

References – because I know you care...

Arango, Tim., Bosman, Julie., Tyalor, Kate. "A Common Trait Among Mass Killers: Hatred Toward Women." *The New York Times*, 2019.

Bellow, Saul. *Humboldt's Gift*. The Alison Press, 1975. Penguin Books, 1978.

Bogle, Eric. "Safe in the Harbour." *When the Wind Blows*, additional performances by John Munro and Brent Miller. Larrikin Records, 1984.

Chesterton, Gilbert Keith. *Heretics*. 1905.

--- . "Utopia of Usurers," "The New Name." *Utopia of Usurers and other Essays*, Boni and Liveright, New York, 1917. Project Gutenberg, 2000.

--- . "III. On Mr. Rudyard Kipling and Making the World Small." *Heretics*, John Lane: The Bodley Head, London, 1905. Project Gutenberg, 1996.

Coleridge, Samuel Taylor. "Chapter 4," "Chapter 13," "Chapter 14." *Biographia Literaria*, 1817, edited by Adam Roberts, Edinburgh University Press, 2014.

--- . *The Friend*. No. 5, London, 1809. Internet Archive, 2012.

Davies, John. "Know Thyself." 1599. *Biographia Literaria*, Project Gutenberg, 2004.

Eliot, Thomas Stearns. "Tradition and the Individual Talent."
    The Egoist, 1919

Girard, René. *Violence and the Sacred.* Editions Bernard Grasset,
    1972. Translated by Patrick Gregory, The John Hopkins
    University Press, 1997.

Hedberg, Mitchell Lee. *Mitch All Together.* 2003.

Hopkins, Gerard Manley. *As Kingfishers Catch Fire.* 1887. Poetry
    Foundation.

Incel. *Merriam-Webster.com Dictionary.*

James, Henry. "The Private Life," "Owen Wingrave." *Ghost Stories
    of Henry James,* Wordsworth Editions, 2001.

Jones, Ernest. "The Oedipus-Complex as An Explanation of
    Hamlet's Mystery: A Study in Motive." *The American Jounral of
    Psychology,* vol. 21, no. 1, January, 1910, 72-113.

Keats, John. "Ode on a Grecian Urn." 1819. Poetry Foundation.

Knightriders. Written and directed by Romero, George A. 1981.

Laertius, Diogenes. *Lives of Eminent Philosophers,* edited by Robert
    Drew Hicks. Perseus Digital Library.

Lawrence, David Herbert. *Why the Novel Matters.* 1936.
    UTORweb.

MacDonald, George. "The New Name." *Unspoken Sermons,* 1867.
    Unspoken Sermons: Series I, II, III, Project Gutenberg, 2005.

Marlowe, Christopher. *The Tragical History of Doctor Faustus*. 1604. ElizabethanDrama.org

Partridge, Eric. *Origins: A Short Etymological Dictionary of Modern English*. Routledge, 1966.

Plato. "Greater Hippias." *Plato in Twelve Volumes*, vol. 9, translated by Walter Rangeley Maitland Lamb. Cambridge, MA, Harvard University Press; London, William Heinemann, 1925. Perseus Digital Library.

Puzo, Mario. The Fortunate Pilgrim. Atheneum Books, New York, 1964. Ballantine Books, New York, 1997.

Ross, James. "Immaterial Aspects of Thought." *The Journal of Philosophy*, vol. 89, no. 3, March 1992, pp 136-150.

Ruskin, John. "The Political Economy of Art." 1858. *Unto This Last, and Other Essays on Political Economy*. Project Gutenberg, 2011.

Shakespeare, William. *Hamlet, Prince of Denmark*. 1623. Project Gutenberg, 1998.

--- . *King Henry the Fourth, the First Part*. 1623. Project Gutenberg, 1998.

--- . *The Merchant of Venice*. 1623. Project Gutenberg, 1998.

---. *The Taming of the Shrew*. 1623. Project Gutenberg, 1998.

Sheen, Fulton John. "The Meaning of Love." *Life is Worth Living*, DuMont Television Network, 1954.

Shelley, Percy Bysshe. "A Defense of Poetry." 1840. *A Defense of Poetry and Other Essays*, Project Gutenberg, 2004.

Skeat, Walter William. *Concise Etymological Dictionary of the English Language*, Perigee Books, 1980.

Steinman, James Richard. "Good girls go to Heaven (Bad Girls go Everywhere)." Original Sin, performed by Pandora's Box, lead vocals by Holly Sherwood. 1989.

---. "Nowhere Fast." performed by Fire Inc., vocals by Rory Dodd, Laurie Sargent, Holly Sherwood, and Eric Troyer. 1984.

---. "Out of the Frying Pan (And into the Fire)," "Objects in the Rear View Mirror may Appear closer than they Are." Bat out of Hell II: Back into Hell, lead vocals by Michael Lee Aday. Ocean Way, Power Station, 1993.

---. "The Artist's Mind." Jimsteinman.com.

---. "Two out of Three Ain't Bad," "Paradise by the Dashboard Light." Bat out of Hell, lead vocals by Michael Lee Aday, the duet cited with vocalist Ellen Foley, produced by Todd Rundgren. Bearsville, Utopia Sound, The Hilt Factory, House of Music, 1997.

The Bible. New International Version, 3rd ed. Biblica, 2011.

Tolkien, John Ronald Ruel. "On Fairy-Stories." *Oxford University Press*, 1947. University of Houston.

Yeats, William Butler. "The Second Coming." *The Dial*, 1920. Poetry Foundation.

Youngman, Hank. *An Essay Concerning Human Misunderstanding.* 2024.

--- . "The Debtor," "The Rambling Apostle." *The Chapbooks Trilogy,* 2023.

--- . *The Playwright.* 2022.

---. *Pythagoras' Prison.* 2022.

<u>In this Series...</u>

<u>*Pythagoras' Prison*</u>

In this introductory essay, the author explains the structure of our conceptual prison, the danger of its illusion, and the circumstances surrounding its creation – ideological, practical, and personal. Through an elaborate metaphor of crime, toymakers, and an asylum, Pythagoras' Prison is written to illustrate the modern fallacy and to refocus the purpose of thought on to its original trajectory.

<u>*An Essay Concerning Human Misunderstanding*</u>

An Essay Concerning Human Misunderstanding is the central entry in the eponymous series. It is a meditation on a selection of contemporary passions that burden the modern citizen. Relying on linguistic science, philosophical appeal, and human curiosity, it locates their origin in a conceptual error, which discovery is at once to the reader's satisfaction and the means of recovery.

<u>*Bards, Robots, and Hordes*</u>

A treatise on defeat as an outcome not at all humiliating: sometimes, it is not triumph that determiners winner from loser. There follow three essays: on art; artificial intelligence; and mankind's regression into the primitive commune known as a horde – an uncaring, uneducated, and untrusting population. It is about deception by ornament, an unusual orphanhood, and conceptual deterioration... a conclusion just shy of optimistic goes without saying.

<u>Also by Hank Youngman...</u>

The Chapbooks Trilogy

A printed collection of 50 poems and 3 essays, divided in three parts according to form and subject matter: _Ambition in Vain_, _Songlets_, and _Chapbook #3_.
Each part can also be purchased independently as a digital copy.

It Comes with the Territory

A science-fiction mystery adventure with an emphasis on the real-world factors that enable the grounds for the plot. Written in the tradition of classic science fiction, _It Comes with the Territory_ aims to entertain, in as far as the reader enjoys mystery adventures, as well as to inspire thought, in as far as the reader is accustomed to thinking.

The Playwright

Set in a plot that is in the same measure natural and supernatural, _The Playwright_ is a unique take on the ghost story as narrated in a modern context – a work of mystery, suspense, and light horror, it is an ideal read for the modern enthusiast of the genre.

A Righteous Agenda

A work of mystery, suspense, and light satire that aims to provide an intriguing set of characters and events, with a twist that is subtly foretold yet remains just out of grasp until the conclusion.